WALKING IN WILLS' SHOES

by

DAVID HILLAN
with YVONNE HILL

Copyright © 2021, 2022 by David Hillan, Yvonne Hill

All rights reserved. No part of this publication may be reproduced, or transmitted, or used in any manner without written permission of the copyright owner, except where permitted by law. All inquiries should be made to the publisher at the address below.

Original Manuscript, *Burke and Wills in the Gulf Country*, by David Hillan 2019 located at John Oxley Library, State Library of Queensland.
First paperback edition 2021. Second paperback edition 2022.

Disclaimer. Although the authors, contributors, and publisher have made every effort to ensure that the information in this book was correct at press time, the authors, contributors, and publisher do not assume and hereby disclaim any liability to any party for any loss, damage, or disruption caused by errors or omissions, whether such errors or omissions result from negligence, accident, or any other cause.

Interior Photographs by Yvonne Hill — © 2022
Cover Design by Yvonne Hill — © 2022
Cover Photo by Rosie Steggles

ISBN 978-0-6487007-3-9

Published by Heart Press
67 Sugars Rd Bellbowrie
QLD 4070
Australia

Dedicated to the memory of
William John Wills 1834–
1861
In recognition of his outstanding abilities as a surveyor

ABOUT THE AUTHORS

David Nathan Hillan
Dip. Surveying, Dip. Town & Regional Planning
1930–2016

The author, David Hillan, became a registered Surveyor in NSW in 1952 and later in other States of Australia. During this time, he was engaged on a wide variety of surveys covering marking original country sections, townships, engineering surveys, air photo control for map making, tunnel alignment surveys and reconnaissance for major projects. The work in marking out sections involved the search for blazed trees of early surveyors from the nineteenth and twentieth centuries. His work on photographic tunnel cross sections won a prestigious award in a professional journal in 1955. This technique has subsequently been used extensively overseas.

In the mid-seventies he developed an original photographic survey method to determine flight paths of aircraft for the control of noise. A paper on this was presented to a Parliamentary Select Committee. He was involved in maritime search and rescue for more than thirty years and some of the techniques used in that activity have been utilised in this investigative research.

In addition, he was an Olympian, having been section manager for his sport at the 1972 Munich and 1976 Montreal Olympic Games as well as manager of many other international teams.

This book was developed from his original manuscript, which was edited, partially re-written and published by his wife, Yvonne, after his death.

Yvonne Avis Hill OAM, OLY

B.A., Dip. T. Sec, Grad. Dip. Ed. Admin.

1937–

Follow along with anecdotes from the long-suffering wife, written in italics.

Co-author and David's wife, Yvonne Hill, worked in South Australian secondary schools for thirty-eight years, retiring as a Class 1 Principal. She is a multi-award-winning photographer and has given more than thirty years voluntary service to the South Australian Sea Rescue Squadron in searches at sea as well as working for seventeen years as chief radio operator during search and rescue operations.

An Olympic target rifle shooter, she was also, for many years, coach for both Olympic and Paralympic shooters. Winner of twenty international medals, including gold and silver at the 1982 World Championships, she was awarded an Order of Australia medal in 2015 for her services to her sport and the community. After retiring from international competition, having competed at the 1980 Olympics in Moscow, the 1982 World Championships in Venezuela, the 1982 Commonwealth Games in Brisbane and also the 1986 World Championships in East Germany, she was manager and/or coach for many overseas teams both Olympic and Paralympic.

She recently retired from the board of Target Rifle Australia and is currently Junior Vice President of the Australian Photographic Society.

yvonnehill.com.au

HOW DID IT ALL COME ABOUT?

Our interest in the story of Burke and Wills was sparked when we were fishing in the Bynoe River in far north Queensland in 1994. One day, the fish were not biting, and David began to speculate how far north Burke and Wills had actually reached — was it that sandhill we could see from our boat?

When we returned home to Adelaide, David began to read and study everything he could find on the story of this ill-fated expedition, which had been tasked with travelling from Melbourne to the Gulf of Carpentaria in a bid to reach the sea before anyone else.

From then on until our last trip in 2012, our main quest was to find the solution to the mystery of what happened north of Camp 119, falsely believed by many to be the Expedition party's last camp. This was not true as Burke and Wills, with minimal rations and just the horse Billy, left the rest of the party at Camp 119 and pushed north for a further three days. Our on-ground research had begun and for the next eighteen years, we walked in the shoes of Wills, the party's surveyor and navigator, solving the mystery of how close they got to the sea.

When we crossed Leichhardt's tracks, we added him to the mysteries to be solved. By the time our trips north had ended, we had found and photographed fifteen of Leichhardt's blazed trees between the Norman and Leichhardt Rivers, using his original notes sourced from the microfiche records in the Mitchell Library in NSW.

Unfortunately, his notes west of the Leichhardt River had been water damaged and were unreadable, otherwise we would have continued. As a surveyor who had worked on the Snowy River Hydro Scheme in the 1950s, David had experience looking for blazed trees left by early surveyors, which helped our searches for trees in the Gulf country. In addition, our lengthy experience in search and rescue at sea, aided our investigations.

—Yvonne Hill

CONTENTS

Introduction i
Acknowledgements v
Chapter 1: The Magnet of the North 1
Chapter 2: Who was William John Wills? 10
Chapter 3: A Series of Errors 13
Chapter 4: The Gossamer Globe 16
Chapter 5: The Gulf Country 28
Chapter 6: Through North Queensland 41
Chapter 7: Technology of the Times 48
Chapter 8: Previous Explorers 61
Chapter 9: Camp 119 80
Chapter 10: Wills' Navigation Skills 86
Chapter 11: Navigation Instruments 91
Chapter 12: To the Last Camp 104
Chapter 13: The Last Camp 132
Chapter 14: Dash to the Sea 145
Chapter 15: Last Words 156
Appendix 1 159
Appendix 2 161
References 169
Notes 173

INTRODUCTION

History can be subjective. It is subject to review and change based on the personal perspective of the historian. Facts become overlooked or distorted in the telling and re-telling of history. People tend to assume that what a historian writes is correct in every respect, because we are unable to go back to original materials or locations and check the facts. But, sometimes, original sources do survive, as I discovered along with my husband David Hillan: -

From 1861–1862, Robert Burke and William Wills set out to find a route from Melbourne to the northern coast of Australia. Wills' notes and survey calculations from this Expedition still exist. Combined with physical evidence at the original location, we can pull back the veil of time and uncover a mystery 160 years old.

A monument to Burke and Wills stands in the Gulf Country of far north Queensland. The iron plaque and inscription mounted on sandstone is set at the site of their Camp 119, located on the Burketown Development Road west of Normanton. Many believe this to be their last northward campsite. But records show that the two intrepid explorers continued north, spending three days trying to reach the Gulf coast. A hundred and sixty years on, not one researcher, apart from myself (David Hillan) with my wife Yvonne Hill, physically retraced their steps in this important section of the journey.

Most research about this Expedition is old and based on even older maps, now primitive in the light of today's technology. Navigating with just the sun, stars and moon was both inaccurate and time consuming. Only in the 1920s did historians discover that Burke and Wills' route did not go through Cloncurry. In fact, it lay many miles to the west. In addition, emerging technology revealed the true locations of features named in Wills' original notes.

Although surveyor Wills left many clues, only another surveyor armed with today's technology could understand them.

Maps today are more accurate than ever with air photos and Global Positioning Systems (GPS) — navigation systems that give your position within a few metres, thanks to satellite data. We can now revise history by incorporating innovative methods to validate Wills' navigation and his achievements. A solution to the mystery of where they were and what they did in those last three days is now within our reach.

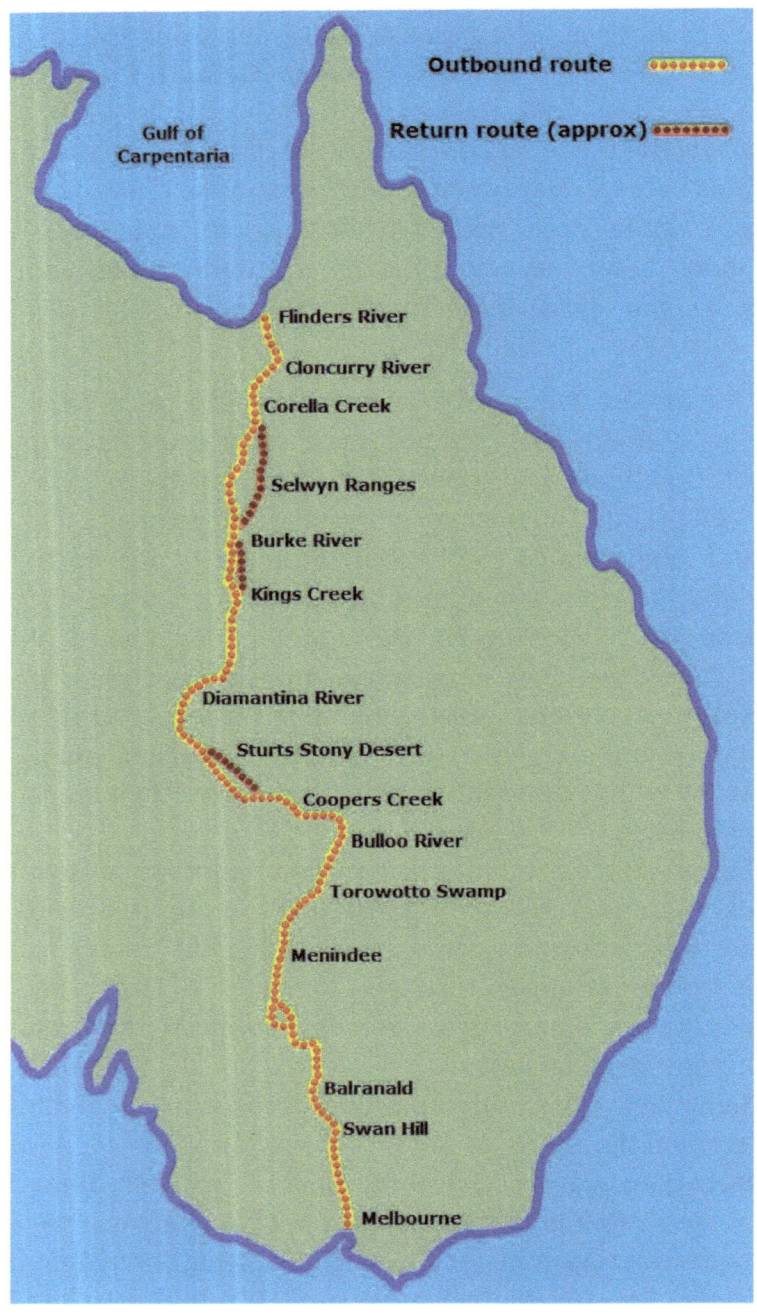

**The route of the Burke and Wills Expedition
Map by Rocketfrog at the English language Wikipedia,
CC BY-SA**[i]

This is Wills' story as told by David Hillan with anecdotes about incidents that occurred during our eighteen years of research added in italics by me, his wife, Yvonne Hill.

David Hillan's original manuscript, named "Burke and Wills in the Gulf Country" resides in the John Oxley Library, which contains collections unique to Queensland, in the State Library of Queensland.

The map on the left shows the route of the Burke and Wills Expedition of 1860–1861, which began from Melbourne in mid-winter. After leaving the other two party members, King and Gray, at Camp 119, Burke and Wills pushed on for a further three days amid the searing heat of a tropical summer in far north Queensland to try to reach the sea.

INTRODUCTION

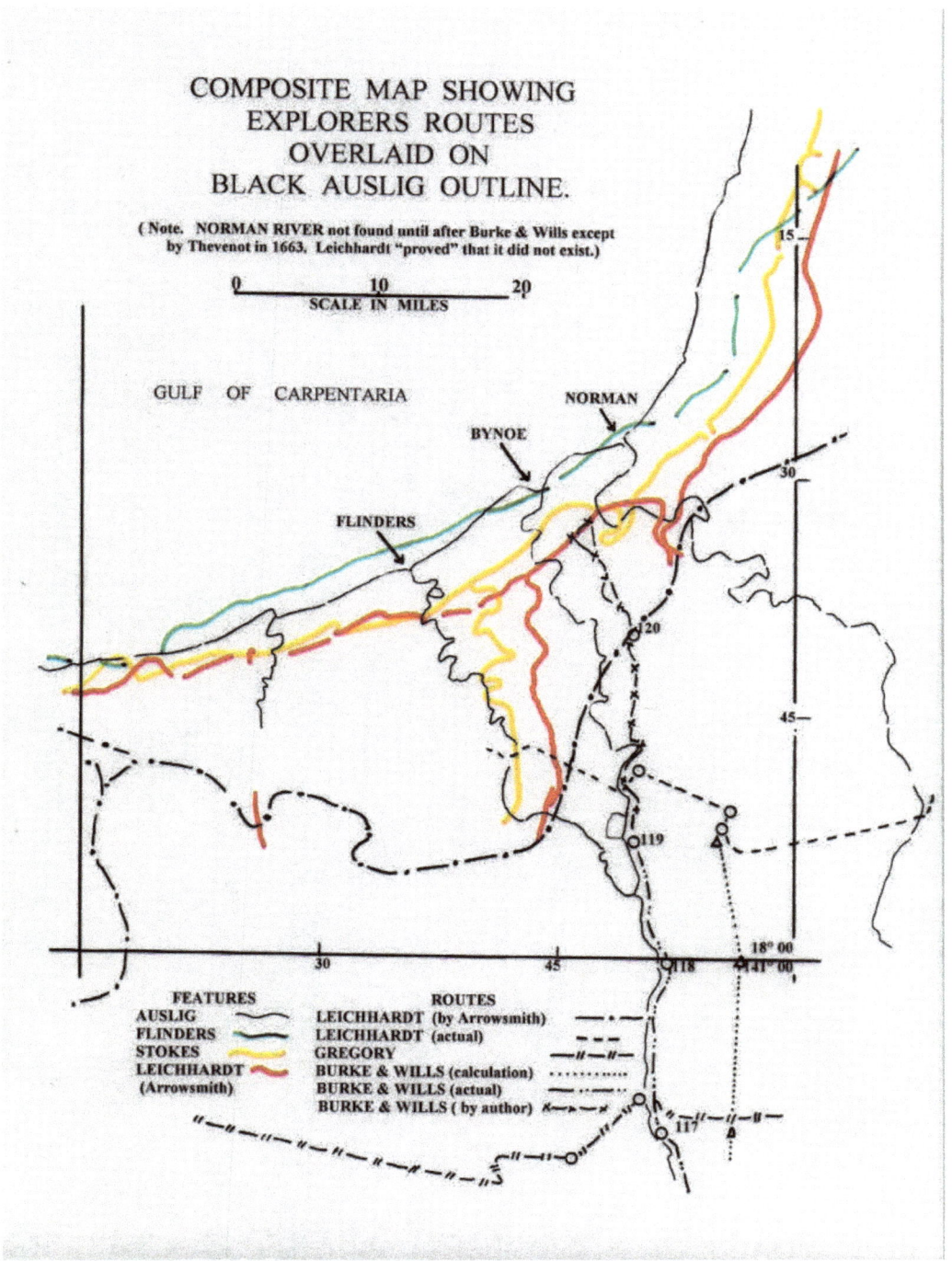

The three rivers named above are keys to their journey

ACKNOWLEDGEMENTS

Our thanks to the owners and managers of the cattle stations across the Gulf Country: -

- Magowra
- Milgarra
- Inverleigh
- Inverleigh West
- Wernadinga

for permission to access their stations and for encouragement and support in our quest.

As well, I would like to acknowledge the valuable assistance given to us in the preparation of this book for publishing by: -

Gill McMillan and Norm Hunter for their expert proofreading

Kyla Jo Magin for her exceptional editing skills

Frank Miller and Ian Manthorpe of SA Sea Rescue Squadron for checking navigation edits for accuracy

and not least my daughter, Jacqueline Hill (artatheart.com.au), for her wonderful assistance and moral support.

CHAPTER 1
THE MAGNET OF THE NORTH

Who would have thought that, at the age of sixty-two, I would find myself perched in a tree in far north Queensland, above a mob of angry wild pigs?

Certainly not me. Though, in retrospect, such challenges were part of undertaking an incredible journey to unravel a mystery. In mid-1860, Robert Burke and William Wills set out with an expedition party from Melbourne into the wilderness of northern Australia. In early February 1861, the pair made a three-day dash north, planning to reach Queensland's Gulf coastline before heading back south. How close they got to the coastline is shrouded in mystery — a mystery we would uncover.

The "we" comprised my retired surveyor and town planner husband, David Hillan, and myself, Yvonne Hill, a photographer and retired high school teacher. I describe myself as the long-suffering wife, but the truth is that I would not have missed the adventure for anything!

On this occasion, we were in a remote corner of a Gulf cattle station on our 4WD motorbike looking for a blazed tree. A fence with no gate and tight wire halted our bike. We gathered up our snacks and water and I grabbed my camera (no self-respecting photographer goes anywhere without a camera). As we walked down the banks of a creek, we could hear the sounds of a mob of wild pigs coming towards us.

Up a tree in far North Queensland

We quickly looked around for a tree to climb and this was the sturdiest we could find. David was over six feet tall and climbed up first before pulling me up behind.

Our pitiful situation was partly of our own making. We had made the cardinal mistake of leaving our rifle on the 4WD bike. After some time, the pigs departed. When silence reigned, I decided to venture down and set my camera on a ten-second delay before placing it on the ground. I got a shot of our predicament that provided a good picture for the Christmas cards that year.

Despite such a moment of terror, both David and I had a great love for the Gulf country. His words below attest to this: -

The Gulf country of far north Queensland and the Northern Territory has always been a magnet to me. Whether it was the remoteness, the mystique or the romance of the area I do not know.

To me, the long-suffering wife, the beauty of the area is in its uniqueness. Amidst vast distances of grey dust and bush lie large cattle stations and down-to-earth people with children who often learn to ride horses before they can walk. The wide-brimmed Australian Akubra is the hat of choice for most people. Families like to get together as often as possible on occasions such as rodeos and camp drafts.

We were invited to the Burketown Ball, which was quite unlike any Ball in a city. Blue jeans were not only acceptable attire, they were expected. Naturally, the children attended too.

CHAPTER 1: THE MAGNET OF THE NORTH

Modern muster methods

History of Gulf Exploration

David grew up in the country and had practised as a surveyor in several remote areas, so he was well-suited to exploring isolated places in the bush. Though, at the start of our journey, we had much to learn.

My knowledge of the area's history was vague. Whether this was due to a fading memory or lack of attention during Australian history lessons in my school days I cannot tell. I certainly had background knowledge of Burke and Wills — and of Ludwig Leichhardt, who, eighteen years earlier, had mapped some of the Gulf area through which Burke and Wills travelled — but that information proved to be very minimal.

I knew nothing of Captain John Lort Stokes, perhaps one the most amazing and professional of all Australian explorers. In the years 1837–1843, while sailing in the *Beagle*, Captain Stokes contributed a great deal to the early exploration of Australia's northern coastal areas. Researchers and navigators still used Stokes's work up until the Second World War. Indeed, much of it can even be found in current nautical charts of the Gulf of Carpentaria. His survey of the coastline was also available to Wills.

Many others explored the Gulf of Carpentaria before Captain Cook arrived in Australia. People from the chain of islands to the north explored the coast by sea with very small craft. They left no legacy of maps, but they did leave evidence of their visits. They sailed south-southeast into a virtual closed sea using the northwest monsoons. A few months later, they returned to their bases with the southeast monsoons.

One of the most famous and well-known of the early navigators was Matthew Flinders. On the 17th of February 1803, Flinders, who commanded the *Investigator* during a major survey of Australia's northern coastline, recorded contact with such a group of vessels near the northeastern tip of Arnhem Land, which he named Malay Road and: -

> ... we learned that they were prows from Macassar, and the six Malay commanders shortly afterwards came on board in a canoe. It happened fortunately that my cook was a Malay, and through his means I was able to communicate with them. The chief of the six prows was a short, elderly man, named Pobassoo; he said there were upon the coast, in different divisions, sixty prows, and that Salloo was the commander in chief. These people were Mahometans, and on looking into the launch, expressed great horror to see hogs there; nevertheless they had no objection to port wine, and even requested a bottle to carry away with them at sunset... [i]
>
> At daylight they got under sail and steered through the narrow passage between Cape Wilberforce and Bromby's Isles, by which we had come; and afterwards directed their course south-eastward into the Gulph of Carpentaria...
>
> According to Pobassoo, from whom my information was principally obtained, sixty prows belonging to the Rajah of Boni, and carrying one thousand men, had left Macassar with the north-west monsoon, two months before, upon an expedition to this coast; and the fleet was then lying in different places to the westward, five or six together, Pobassoo's division being the foremost. These prows seemed to be about twenty-five tons, and to have twenty- or twenty-five men in each; that of Pobassoo carried two small brass guns, obtained from the Dutch, but

others had only muskets; besides which, every Malay wears a cress or dagger, either secretly or openly...

The object of their expedition was a certain marine animal, called trepang. Of this they gave me two dried specimens; and it proved to be beche-de-mer, or sea cucumber... [ii]

Flinders recorded that the visitors' navigated with knowledge of the seasonal winds, aided by a very small pocket compass but "without the aid of any chart or astronomical observation." Centuries of passed-down experience contributed to Pobassoo's detailed knowledge, including that "the north-west monsoon... would not blow quite a month longer.[iii]" Flinders could confirm Pobassoo's information about lost craft as he had recently found some of the relics.

In 1605 the *Duyfken* brought the first of several Dutch explorers. In 1642, Abel Tasman travelled in the *Limmen* and produced an extremely detailed chart that named Gulf features. More than a hundred and fifty years after the Dutch, Flinders explored the area from 1801–1803 in the *Investigator*. Then, between 1837–1843, Captain Stokes produced the most thorough mapping to that date while sailing in the *Beagle*.

The *Stad Amsterdam*, a Dutch replica tall ship that visited Australia in 2010; it would have been similar to the *Duyfken*

Next came the land explorers. The first was Leichhardt, from 1844–1845, on his successful expedition from near Brisbane to Port Essington — an isolated port on the Cobourg Peninsula northeast of the current-day Darwin city. This settlement was abandoned a few years later. In 1855–1856, Augustus Gregory appeared on the scene. He travelled west to east, skirting south of the boggy coastal Gulf plains that Leichhardt had noted.

Then came Burke and Wills in February 1861. From Melbourne, the Expedition travelled across the continent to the northern area of the Gulf of Carpentaria. Within a year, three separate land expeditions led by Frederick Walker, John McKinlay and William Landsborough searched for Burke and Wills. Captain Norman supported these searches in the ship *Victoria*, temporarily based at the Albert River and Sweers Island. The Norman River was later named after the captain, and the nearby Sweers Island bears the lonely grave of one of his crew, Gunner James Frost who was accidentally killed on the 31st of December 1861. (See below.)

CHAPTER 1: THE MAGNET OF THE NORTH

Like most tourists who travel through the area, my interest in its history was general and low key. My lack of knowledge on the subject was extensive, but I soon discovered that I was not alone in this deficiency.

Over our journey, we learnt not just about the history of the land but about its people. While driving on remote tracks in far north Queensland, we met stockmen herding cattle alongside the road (in the so-called long paddock) as well as tourists. This was in the dry season when feed was scarce, but some feed could still be found on the roadsides. Naturally, the cattle had right of way, and we always pulled off the road to let them pass.

On one of our trips north when we stopped for a herd of cattle, I climbed up on top of the 4WD bike on the back of the truck, which was my usual perch for taking photographs. One of the cattle dogs decided to clamber up over the wheel arch and get up on my lap for a cuddle. I apologised to the stockman as I knew it was a working dog, but he assured me that his kids played with the dogs at home all the time, so it was OK. That was probably the moment I fell in love with those clever dogs.

Thirsty working dogs drinking from the stockman's hat on the side of the road

The First Question

Roper Bar in the Northern Territory sits near the most downstream crossing point on the Roper River and close to the temporary port used during the construction of part of the overland telegraph line, which crossed Australia from south to north. The area is also steeped in the history of Leichhardt's endeavours. The Roper Bar was a staging camp for the enigmatic bushman, Andrew Hume, while he attempted to locate any survivors from Leichhardt's ill-fated final expedition.

There we met a fellow traveller who advised us to keep a lookout, as we headed south and east, for Burke and Wills' last campsite. The turnoff, he told us, was just after the Little Bynoe River crossing a few kilometres west of Normanton. The instructions duly followed, we arrived at the site with its blazed tree and monument. I noted that the signage labelled the site as the last northern camp of Burke and Wills. However, I knew that they had spent three days north of that point.

How then could this be their last camp? I had asked my first question and unbeknown to me I was becoming committed to an intriguing trail of research.

In the following weeks, I fished and explored the lower section of the Bynoe River well north of its junction with Saltwater Creek (see map on page iii). The Norman River is further east. These rivers are separated by a strip of land, at the northern end, from about six to thirteen kilometres wide running down to the Gulf just west of Karumba. Burke and Wills had spent their final three days in that area. What had they achieved on this isolated stretch of land?

Fishing is not an occupation that keeps you busy, so I had plenty of time to think and speculate on all manner of things. Often, I found myself looking at the nearby riverbanks and wondering if Burke and Wills had once walked along that sand hill. Perhaps they had been turned back by the river right there? My curiosity led me to explore by boat, Russell Creek, a tributary of the Norman River, during high tides for about thirteen kilometres (eight miles) at the northeast corner of the Stokes Range. This in turn prompted further speculation.

The source of my topographical information was the AUSLIG map sheet MAGOWRA 1:100 000.

AUSLIG was the Australian Surveying and Land Information Group, which merged with the Australian Geological Survey Organisation in 2001 to become Geoscience Australia. Its main function was to provide national geographic information. This included producing up-to-date topographical maps at various scales covering the whole of Australia. It also provided satellite imagery to industry and government.

CHAPTER 1: THE MAGNET OF THE NORTH

David in deep thought, no doubt thinking about Burke and Wills

My basic curiosity led me to embark on a search of the literature for information after returning home to Adelaide, more than three thousand kilometres south. I soon realised that there was no simple answer. No one had yet researched the subject to a logical conclusion. I found conflicting opinions as well as controversial ones. Trying to solve this mystery become an obsession for me over the next eighteen years.

Many answers that I found in this initial research were clearly incorrect. A typical claim was that Burke and Wills "mistook the river they were on for the Albert"; another, "they knew not where they were"; yet another; "they mistook Magnetic for True North". The Government Astronomer recalculated two of Wills' points near the northern end, but these recalculations can easily be shown as wrong. Easily that is with today's information and technology. The Government Astronomer along with other experts of the time were unable to accurately check their calculations as I could.

At first, I did not think much about these many negative answers without a single positive one. Then I started to take a deeper look and realised that a lot of their journey was misunderstood. What did Burke and Wills achieve in the Gulf country? As this is an important part of Australia's history and of local history, I was determined to uncover the truth.

CHAPTER 2
WHO WAS WILLIAM JOHN WILLS?

Burke is pictured left, Wills on the right

The simple answer is that he was the surveyor appointed to guide an expedition from Melbourne to the northern sea at the Gulf of Carpentaria. The South Australian Government had offered a prize for the first team to cross the continent from south to north. The Victorians raced to reach the goal before South Australia and thus open the Australian interior for future settlement.

Initially, the expedition was known as the Victorian Exploring Expedition. Robert O'Hara Burke was the appointed leader, but with the resignation of his second-in-command and the dwindling numbers in the expedition party, Wills became Burke's deputy. Over the journey, he also proved himself a competent navigator. Quite rightly, the expedition came to be known as the Burke and Wills Expedition.

Wills was much more than just a surveyor. We can understand the man he was by reading his father's dedication (see next page). It reveals a young man who became a highly competent navigator, who paid attention to detail and who diligently recorded his work and the journey they made. A youthful illness left him a little slow in speech but certainly not in intellect. He deliberated before he spoke and, when he did, he presented a thoughtful and intelligent consideration of the matter at hand.

He spent the first seventeen years of his life with his family in the small English town of Totnes in Devon, receiving an education and developing an interest in things scientific and technical. In 1852, at age eighteen, William Wills and his younger brother Thomas set sail for Australia where they were later joined by their father.

Initially Wills was apprenticed to his father, who was a doctor, and gained some knowledge of medicine. Later, at a relatively young age — in his mid-twenties — he became a proficient and respected surveyor in Victoria. The fact that he had no difficulty, despite the unknown and forbidding territory, in finding the best route to the northern coast and back again to Cooper's Creek, speaks for itself. The success or otherwise of the Expedition rested largely on his shoulders.

Was this Expedition a success or failure? We set out to solve this very mystery.

Words From a Father

Wills is best described in the preface to his biography, written by his father: -

> A life terminating before it had reached its meridian, can scarcely be expected to furnish materials for an extended biography. But the important position held by my late son, as second in command in what is now so well-known as the Burke and Wills Exploring Expedition across the Island Continent of Australia; the complicated duties he undertook as Astronomer, Topographer, Journalist, and Surveyor; the persevering skill with which he discharged them, suggesting and regulating the march of the party through a waste of eighteen hundred miles, previously untrodden by European feet; his courage, patience, and heroic death; his self-denial in desiring to be left alone in the desert with scarcely a hope of rescue, that his companions might find a chance for themselves; these claims on public attention demand that his name should be handed down to posterity in something more than a mere obituary record, or an official acknowledgment of services.
>
> A truthful, though brief, memoir of my son's short career, may furnish a stimulating example, by showing how much can be accomplished in a few years, when habits of prudence and industry have been acquired in early youth. He fell a victim to errors not originating with himself; but he resigned his life without a murmur,

having devoted it to science and his country. His death, with the circumstances attending it, furnishes an application of the lines of a favourite poet, which he often quoted with admiration:

> Lives of great men all remind us
> We can make our lives sublime,
> And departing leave behind us
> Footsteps on the sands of time;
> Footprints that perhaps another,
> Sailing o'er Life's solemn main,
> A forlorn and shipwreck'd brother,
> Seeing, shall take heart again.

Wills' favourite poet was Henry Wadsworth Longfellow, the author of this poem.

CHAPTER 3
A SERIES OF ERRORS

In 1922 Robert Logan Jack, a former Government Geologist, published a comprehensive book in two volumes covering explorations in far north Queensland. However, he treated Burke and Wills' exploration as a peripheral item.[i]

Logan Jack illustrated his book with eighteen detailed plans (also known as plots) showing all explorers' routes in the area. His illustration of Burke and Wills' route near Cloncurry was miles out; he showed them passing through where the town of Cloncurry now lies on the Cloncurry River — a river named by Burke and Wills in their notes.

But Burke and Wills did not actually travel along the Cloncurry River. They were further west on what is now known as the Corella River. That aside, Logan Jack's plotting of Burke and Wills' route north of Camp 119 is, I believe, perfectly accurate. The only other error was when he failed to identify the fact that they crossed the Saltwater/Magowra Creek.

Current maps and Will's notes show that they must have crossed this creek. Logan Jack's book title asserts his research was written "in the light of modern charting". The book's maps were based on Lands Department maps and Admiralty charts — the best information at the time of publication. Undoubtedly, those maps were assembled from many sources of varying reliability. We can now identify many errors in the topographical information of that time through current charting, with the explorer's original notes together with our on-site research.

In 1862, a book was published in Germany titled *Expedition Unter Burke*. It contained a map that showed an estimate of Burke and Wills' three-day route north of Camp 119. The northernmost point identified in this book is similar to Logan Jack's research.

Current Tools for Today's Researcher

Burke and Wills' route is not the only route past researchers have plotted incorrectly. Researchers, using current technology such as satellite images, can now re-plot early explorers' routes. Doing so with other explorers' routes would be a very fruitful and enlightening field of research; many gross errors I found relating to Burke and Wills' route would be reflected in the records of other explorers.

From 1931 the Army Survey Corps made significant use of aerial photography[ii]. Only in 1942, when Australia was under threat of invasion, did aerial mapping of the Gulf country commence. Maps were produced at a scale of 4 miles to 1 inch[iii] and were a vast improvement on the 1922 maps. But they were still inferior to those available today.

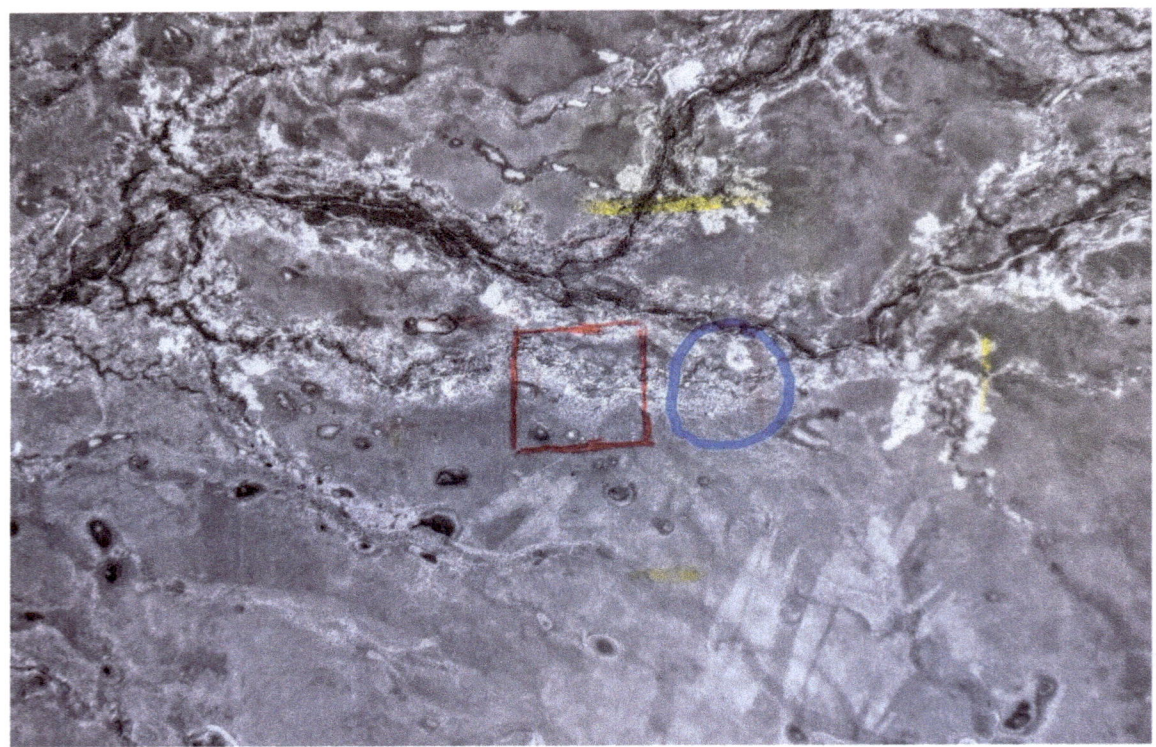

An air photo with an area for investigation marked by David

Interestingly, during our travels in the Gulf country, we located a large wartime airstrip close to the coast along with machine-gun bunkers and empty fuel drums (see next page). The strip is in good condition and I would not be surprised if it is still listed as an emergency landing place for commercial aircraft.

CHAPTER 3: A SERIES OF ERRORS

Bunker complete with machine gun mount

Burke and Wills' route on those three days north of Camp 119 in February 1861 remains a mystery due to several factors: the remoteness of and difficulty accessing the area, early researchers' lack of survey expertise, inaccuracies of early maps and charts and also lack of satellite positioning systems. Now, with little technical expertise, one can accurately and quickly determine latitudes and longitudes using GPS. This ability combined with a surveyor's practical experience can once and for all answer the question: how close did Burke and Wills get to the northern coast?

CHAPTER 4
THE GOSSAMER GLOBE

Speaking of gossamer reminds me of riding our four-wheel drive motorbike through the bush. David was usually the driver with me, the long-suffering wife, riding pillion. My job was to watch out for the gossamer threads of the orb weaver spider. This spider nearly always chose to build its web in the very spot between the bushes or trees where we wanted to drive. Meeting those gossamer threads and their occupant face to face was never a pleasant experience.

When we first began unravelling the mystery of the tragic Burke and Wills' Expedition in the Gulf country, we would trek through the wild bush on foot. Long walks are said to be good for your health! Perhaps that is why David lasted until he was eighty-six and I am still going at eighty-three. We were, of course, a lot younger when we began our quest.

Orb weaver spider

Walking over rough country in far north Queensland required good boots and equally good socks as well as considerable stamina. One fine hot day we walked nearly twenty kilometres, but it was purgatory for David — as you'll see in his next entry. When we went back home to Adelaide, the first thing we did was buy a four-wheel drive motorbike, known hereafter as a 4WD bike.

CHAPTER 4: THE GOSSAMER GLOBE

GOLAH, the 4WD Bike

Why a 4WD bike? One day we walked twenty kilometres across black soil plains, traversing cracks over five centimetres wide that threatened ankle injury. To compound the problem my favourite long-serving lace-up boots had died a few days before. In Normanton, the nearest town within five-hundred kilometres, the only replacement boots available were elastic-sided riding boots. These turned out to be monsters as they devoured my socks in less than a hundred metres. We developed a procedure where I would sit down with my rucksack still on and Yvonne would pull my boots off. I would pull the socks up and then put the boots back on. After walking another hundred metres, we had to stop and repeat the procedure again. This routine quickly became dreaded, made worse by the fact that we did not reach our objective.

The upside was that we invested in a better and safer way to carry out our research.

We decided that just one 4WD bike would do the trick for us both if it were sufficiently large. Our choice was a POLARIS Sportsman 500: an automatic vehicle with 4WD on demand via a thumb switch. We kitted it out so that it suited our requirements perfectly. (See Appendix 1.)

I named it Golah, after one of the camels on the Burke & Wills Expedition.

And so, to the gossamer globe…

To understand the story of Burke and Wills' Expedition, we need to understand in detail how latitudes and longitudes work. This reveals the difficulties of navigation, particularly around the time of the original Expedition.

To the layperson, this system can be confusing at first. But, the method Wills used to record their journey is relatively simple and has been used for hundreds of years.

What are Latitudes and Longitudes?

Imagine Earth as a desk globe that spins on an axis.

The horizontal lines, like the one at the equator, are the lines of latitude, also called parallels of latitude. The vertical lines are lines of longitude, also called meridians of longitude. Latitudes and longitudes give us a way of registering locations all over the globe. For example:

Latitude 27° S, Longitude 153° E (latitude 27 degrees south, longitude 153 degrees east) gives the approximate location of Brisbane, Australia.

CHAPTER 4: THE GOSSAMER GLOBE

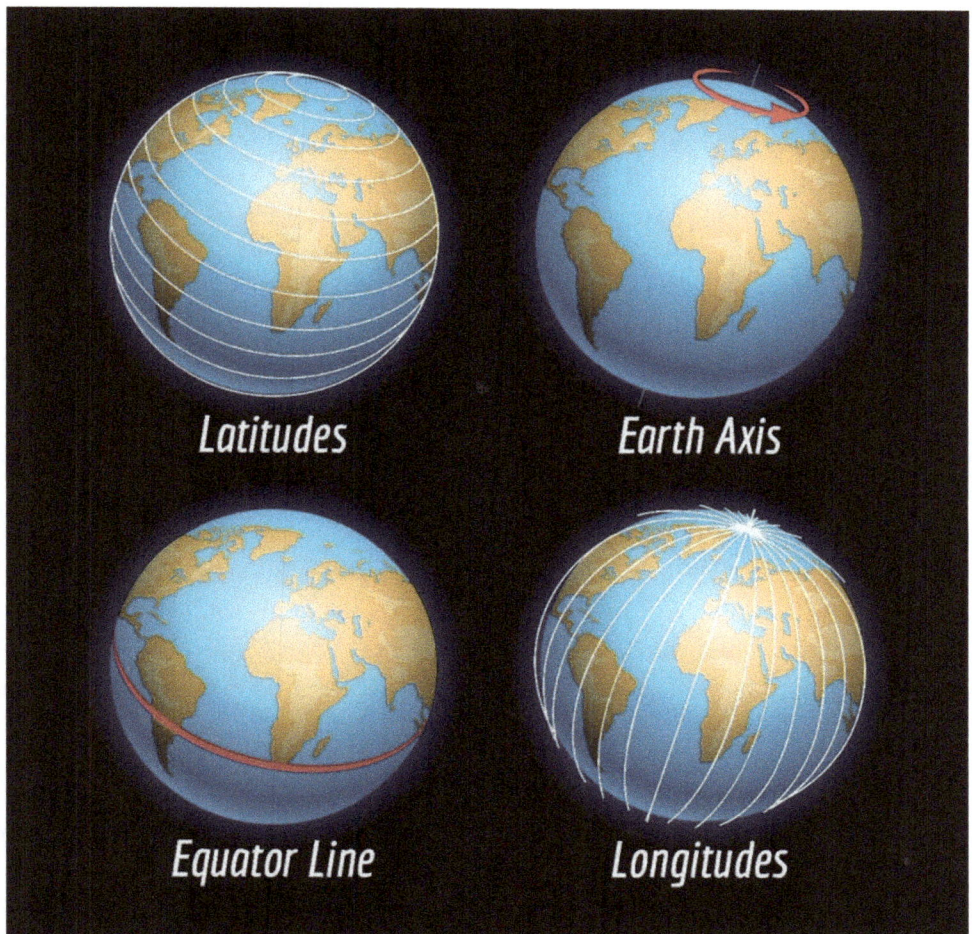

Another view of the gossamer globe

Lines of latitude are the same distance apart.

Lines of longitude, however, are different. The distance between them changes — they are close together near to the North Pole, then steadily widen between there and the equator, then come close together and converge at the south pole.

There are 360 of these longitude lines, one for each of the 360 degrees of a circle. The shape between each pair of lines, if you cut it off the surface of globe and laid it out flat on the table, would look a little like the shape on the left.

Understanding Latitude

If the horizontal lines of latitude are added to our longitude shape, it looks like our new shape on the right.

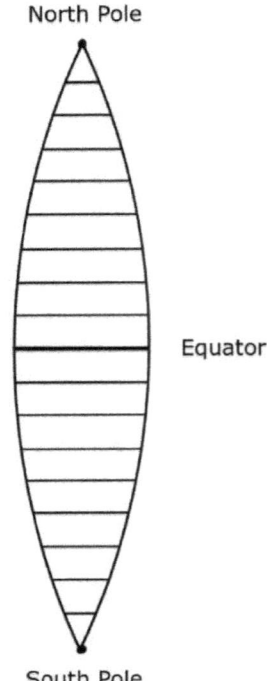

How are horizontal lines of latitude defined? The zero degree (starting point) is at the equator (in the middle) and we then measure up (north) or down (south) from the equator. We know that latitudes are parallel with each other, therefore the distance between any pair of latitudes is always the same wherever they are on the globe.

To explain this further, let's return to our desk globe. Imagine we cut the globe in half from the North pole to the South Pole and anchored a piece of string where the centre of the ball was (the Earth's centre point). Then we stretch the string out and, using a protractor, measure each degree and mark where it lands on the Earth's surface. The equator is at zero degrees, so this is where we match up the 0° on the protractor. The North Pole is 90° north from the equator, and the South Pole is 90° south.

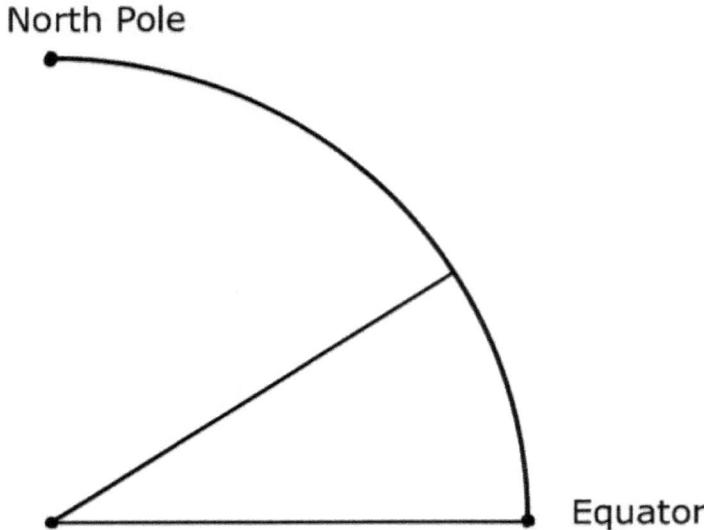

For smaller measurements, we can break down each degree of latitude and longitude into sixty smaller segments, called "minutes". Each degree contains sixty minutes.

It is important to remember that we are measuring angles so far.

In terms of distance across the Earth's surface, one minute of latitude (in a north–south direction) equals one nautical mile.

Using terms of the distances that we are all familiar with, this means: -

1 minute of latitude (north–south) equals =
1 nautical mile
1.15 standard miles (also known as statute miles)
1.85 kilometres

We can break down the minutes of latitude to smaller segments again, called "seconds". Each minute of latitude contains sixty seconds.

If we need even smaller segments, we can break down the minutes and seconds into decimals or fractions, in the same way that time or imperial measurements are noted. For example, ¾ or 0.75 of an accurate position for a latitude can be written as: -

47° 38' 25.75" N (degrees, minutes, decimal seconds) or
47. 6405 N (decimal degrees)

for a latitude of 47 degrees, 38 minutes, 25.75 seconds of angle, north of the equator.

Finding Your Latitude

For the latitude lines, travelling north–south, it was easy for navigators to find their location — even when on a ship that was moving on the sea.

First, we need a starting point, or latitude zero. We've already identified this as the equator, and from there we measure angles north or south towards the poles.

To calculate your angle (the number of degrees can be converted to distance later) away from the equator, all navigators needed to know was where the sun rose and set. Navigators have used this technique for centuries and, with some simple calculations and by factoring in the time of year, they can identify their latitude location with certainty.

Understanding Longitude

It is not as easy to work out where you are currently located on the globe in terms of longitude, i.e., how far around the globe you have travelled in an east–west direction.

To measure angles, you need a starting point to place zero. For latitudes, measuring is done from the equator. But what about longitudes?

Imagine looking at our desk globe from above, directly facing the North Pole. We see the lines of longitude like this: -

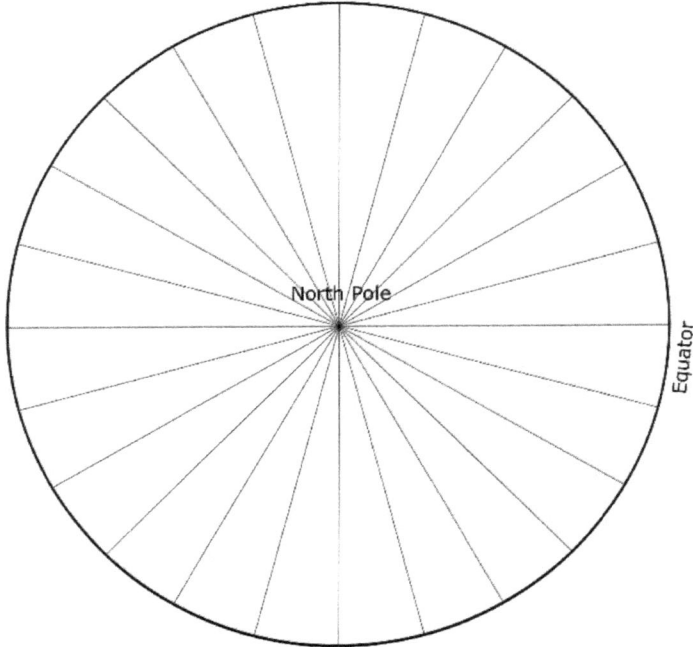

You could lay a circular protractor (or compass — see page 27) over this to measure angles. As a circle, we have 360 degrees of angle around the globe. But we still need to decide on a start point.

Which line of longitude will we pick as the zero position for all of our angles?

Historic Disagreements

In the past this was a political problem. Many countries thought that the world started at their doorstep, i.e., where they were located should be longitude zero and the point from where all longitudes should be measured from. Different starting points caused much confusion and affected the early exploration of Australia.

Both English and French navigators were active in Australia during these early years, and they produced charts centred on London or Paris, respectively[*]. French charts show their longitude of 140° (from Paris) passing through the tip of Cape York

---

[*] These French charts are important parts of Australia's history. One example of this is "Carte Generale de L'Australie", which was a map drawn by V.A. Malte-Brun in July 1863 and published in Paris the following year. This was the map used by Ernst Favenc as a lift out in his publication "The History of Australian Exploration". Another example is the chart of A.H. Dufour titled "Nouvelle Holland ou Australie".

whereas English, and current-day, charts mark their 140° longitude (from London) near the centre of the Gulf of Carpentaria.

If you set your protractor on a map with the 0° (which is also 360°) set on London, all the longitudes in the world can now be read off from that point. If you place it with the 0° anchored on Paris, each degree now marks a different point on our globe. This caused confusion when an English navigator made calculations from a French-made chart and vice versa.

Eventually all countries agreed to start longitude lines from the old observatory site at Greenwich in London. With a common starting point, maps became more accurate across all countries.

Finding Your Longitude with Time

For centuries astronomers, scientists and navigators attempted to use the location of stars and the moon to determine their location. It involved hours of calculations. An alternative method was found that was much simpler. It depended on using the time of day.

If a navigator could know the current time of day wherever they were, and at the same time know the time at the zero point, then they could calculate how far around the globe they had travelled.

Why is that?

Because our world is spinning, time is constantly changing from point to point.

If we know the exact time at both our starting point (longitude 0°) and our current location, we can then work out exactly where we are on the surface of the earth in terms of longitude (i.e., how far around the globe we have travelled).

Here's what we know:
- There are 360 lines of longitude (the same as the number of degrees in a circular protractor).
- The earth rotates once every 24 hours.

This means that each hour of time is equivalent to 15° of longitude (divide 24 into 360).

If we spin our desk globe 15° around its axis, we have a one-hour time difference. Every 1 degree of longitude equates to four minutes of time.

15 degrees of longitude	1 hour of time	Approx. 1600km at the equator, less as you go north or south
1 degree of longitude	4 minutes of time	Approx. 111 km at the equator or 60 nautical miles, less as you go north or south

If it is midday at Greenwich, it will be 1pm at any point on the line of longitude that sits 15 degrees east of Greenwich.

The Chronometer

To find our longitude, we need to know only two times. The time at Greenwich, and the time where we are currently. In the early years, inconsistent and poor-quality watches did not keep time well and made navigators' observations inaccurate.

In the year 1730, while the astronomers and scientists were struggling to locate longitude by moon and stars, a man called John Harrison started working on a special timepiece. He designed and built a device that had two clocks, able to record the time accurately in two places.

He needed his device to be accurate even under temperature or barometric pressure changes and with the movement of a ship. He developed several models over a few decades, until in 1757 he had one that was small and light enough for a sailor to hold in his hand.

By 1815 thousands of chronometers were in use aboard ships across the world. Finally, a navigator on board a ship could measure his longitude.

The Difficulties with Longitude Measurements

There are two problems: -
1. The distances between longitude lines vary as you go north or south, and
2. The problem with reading flat maps of a curved globe.

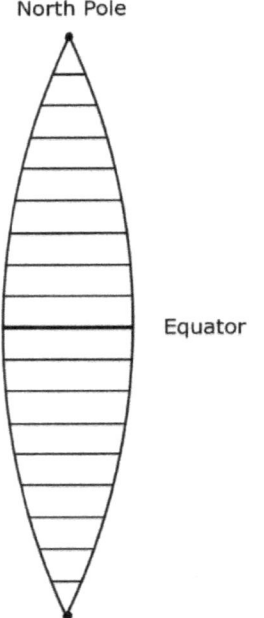

When moving in a north–south direction, measuring distance is easy because all the horizontal (parallel) lines of latitude are the same distance apart.

If we are moving in an east–west direction, for example along the equator (or following any line of latitude), it is a little different.

The nearer to the poles you happen to be, the closer together the lines of longitude are. Remember our flattened-out segment between two lines of longitude (shown on the left).

Along with the varying distances between each line of longitude, other problems creep in because we depict the curved surface of our Earth on a flat map or chart. These issues make it more complicated to measure and identify your location.

There is a third problem as well. The Earth bulges slightly at the equator, which is not necessary to take into account in normal survey and mapping work. We will ignore this.

Charting Your Way

For convenience, the compass can be read in both directions, i.e., both east and west of Greenwich out to 180°. For example, the area of the Gulf of Carpentaria where Burke and Wills travelled is located at about 140°E (east).

As the whole of Australia is east of Greenwich, I will omit the E in future references. Similarly, I will omit the S (south) from latitudes since I will be referring only to locations south of the equator.

Latitude and longitude lines are drawn on the margins of all navigation maps and charts for easy and accurate plotting. Maps and charts are flat versions of the globe, although sea captains often carried a globe for reference as well as charts.

Navigators can calculate the distance and direction between two locations by subtracting the two longitudes and also the two latitudes.

Let us look at an example. Say we have two locations in Australia, location A and location B, with latitudes of: -

Location A	17° 37' 45"
Location B	17° 45' 27"

Location A is showing a latitude of 17 degrees 37 minutes 45 seconds (south). Location B is showing a latitude of 17 degrees 45 minutes 27 seconds (south).

Distance Between Latitudes

Already we know that location B is south of A, because the latitude number is bigger.

Latitude lines start at 0° along the equator and count up going north and also going south i.e., numbers get bigger as we move further away from the equator.

But how much further south is B from A?

Subtract the two latitudes and the difference is 7' 42". This means B is 7' 42" south of A. We can convert this to a distance measurement at the rate of one nautical mile per minute latitude. B is approximately fourteen kilometres (see conversion chart on page 21) south of A.

If point B is not due south of A, another calculation is required to determine the distance and bearing (direction) between them.

And So to Longitudes

In order to calculate differences in longitudes we must scale the distance off the latitudes because the distance between longitude lines decreases the closer you get to the North or South Pole.

A navigator has two methods to read off a map in order to know where to move to next.

Triangle & Trigonometry

The distance between longitudes can be calculated using trigonometry. Each portion of the segment can be regarded as a triangle and, using trigonometry mathematics, the distance and angle can be calculated.

Navigators never chart their locations using this method. Trigonometry is only used in specialist applications, such as Geodesy*.

Distance & Bearing by Protractor

Navigators instead use the protractor method. With this method, it takes two simple steps to find both the distance and the angle between two locations from the map or chart.

1. First, the distance is found by measuring between the two locations on the map and the real-life distance is worked out using the map scale.
2. Then a protractor is used to find the angle between the two locations.

Angles, Bearings & Directions

In surveying and navigation language, the word bearing is often interchanged for the word angle. The bearing is the angle for how far we turn from the north or south direction before we start heading along our track to the destination.

Navigation from one point to the next is often described as a "distance and bearing". This means the distance we travel and the direction we travel in. The bearing is simply an angle away from north (or south as the case may be).

The compass image ("Rose") is often printed on the face of nautical charts for that purpose. Thus, we have the term "compass bearing", which measures an angle away from north.

---

* Geodesy is a branch of Applied Mathematics studying accurate mapping or positioning of points on the globe — especially in relation to large tracts of country and the size, shape and curvature of the earth.

CHAPTER 4: THE GOSSAMER GLOBE

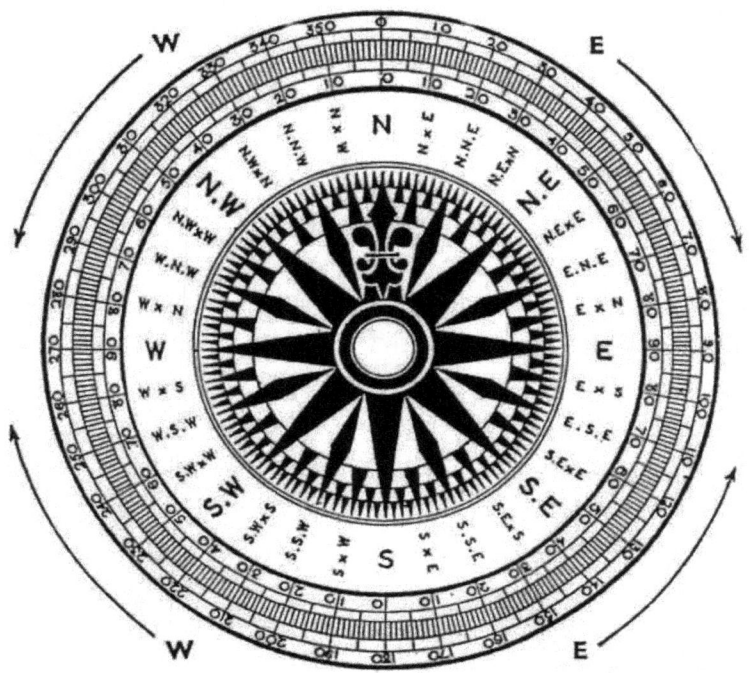

A compass rose often seen on nautical charts

Calculating Early Explorers' Routes

When early explorers such as Burke and Wills recorded their positions by latitude and longitude, they lived in a very different world of navigation. The latitudes and longitudes recorded in the 1860s for each location do not align with current charts and maps. Shifting lines of longitude compounded with slight inaccuracies due to hand-calculated distances presented a challenge for retracing Burke and Will's journey.

But past errors can be recalculated and, armed with the knowledge described in this chapter, I set out to eliminate decades of misconceptions.

CHAPTER 5
THE GULF COUNTRY

In trying to solve our mystery, we explored the most northern reaches of the extensive Gulf river and creek systems. We covered over twenty-six miles* in a straight north–south line on almost flat country, bordering the river and its associated mangrove system. The whole of this distance, except for the first three quarters of a mile, lies north of the Burketown–Normanton road (Burketown Development Road). Camp 119 is located a short distance south of this road. Very few station tracks lie anywhere near the area of interest, and these are not open to the public. But we were fortunate to develop good relationships with station owners and managers. We later shared with them details and photographs of our findings.

Sarus Cranes, sometimes mistaken for Brolgas, on the Burketown Development Road

---

* Due to the historical nature of this research, I will use the same Imperial distance measurements Wills used: -
      1 mile = 0.87 Nautical Mile = 1.61 Kilometres.
      1 Minute of Latitude = 1 Nautical Mile.
Tide and land heights remain metric as they were not referred to by Wills.

CHAPTER 5: THE GULF COUNTRY

When we first travelled the Burketown Development Road, it was little better than a narrow, rough dirt track. Banks of grass more than a metre and a half high hid the world around us as we travelled across the plain in an almost straight line.

We met just one vehicle on our way from Burketown to Normanton, a distance of some two hundred and twenty kilometres: a gaudily painted hippy van complete with hippy dressed in a kaftan.

Naturally, on remote country tracks we always stopped to talk to passers-by. The young man asked us what Burketown was like, saying that Karumba, a further seventy kilometres north of Normanton, was a small town of little interest and with few facilities. We told him that we thought Burketown was good and that we had been able to find a part to repair our vehicle, which was surprising at that time in such a remote location.

When we reached Karumba and found a town about twice the size of Burketown with many more facilities, we wondered what the young hippy would think when he got to Burketown!

Some areas we explored contained mangrove swamps. Driving along the edges of mangrove swamps is the last thing anyone would wish to attempt in a vehicle. It is a recipe for disaster. When driving in the bush I always treated the vehicle with the respect necessary to drive me out. This policy saved time, money, effort and inconvenience — not to mention the possible embarrassment of being stranded.

This policy failed me only once in the 1950s when I worked as a surveyor on the Snowy Mountains Hydro Scheme. I was just one hundred yards short of the road, stuck in a combination of black soil and snow. My 4WD vehicle was in so deep with a broken winch that three bulldozers became bogged trying to get it out. I was certainly not going to tempt the record in the boggy saline black soil near mangroves. Especially not in an extremely isolated location, risking possible property damage and embarrassment to myself.

Unfortunately for David, after he wrote the above words, he did break his record in the Gulf country. It happened late in the afternoon, while riding our 4WD bike north of Camp 120, heading towards the coast. We were approaching a low sandhill and I got off and walked over the nearby sandhill, hoping to get a view of the sea from its top. David continued riding around the end of the sandhill and drove straight into a mangrove swamp, well and truly bogging the bike. He blamed the blunder on driving into the setting sun wearing sunglasses. Because the tide was coming in, this necessitated an extremely fast hike to where the bigger 4WD drive Nissan was parked, about ten kilometres away.

David with bogged vehicle in the Snowy Mountains

After driving back to the stranded bike and hooking it up with a strong wire cable, I was charged with the task of driving out the Nissan while David manoeuvred the bike. Victory was brief for, although David was able to get the bike out, I managed to bog the Nissan. We gathered up our possessions and rode the bike back to the station, some thirty kilometres away. There we waited for the Manager to finish his day's work before returning with us to the bogged vehicle and pulling out the Nissan with his work utility. How embarrassing. Not something we were keen to repeat, particularly as we did not wish to cause any trouble for busy station people.

Traversing the wilderness has other dangers as well. At one stage we ran out of drinking water and had to drink water from melted ice that we had luckily brought in our lunch box. Having said that, I always had complete faith in David, whether in the bush or at sea, and I had no fear about travelling with him into the unknown.

CHAPTER 5: THE GULF COUNTRY

Where is Camp 120?

Finding the location of Burke and Wills' most northern Camp 120 was the major interest in my research. This was where they stayed two nights after leaving the rest of the Expedition party at Camp 119 to make a push towards the sea.

The general area where we knew Camp 120 lay is bounded on the west by the Bynoe River and its tributary Saltwater Creek, along with the upper reaches of Saltwater Creek (which then becomes Magowra Creek further south), and to the east by the Norman River. The southern end of the area that is adjacent to the Burketown road is about twenty-two miles from Normanton, whilst the northern end is just across the Norman River from Karumba. (See map below.)

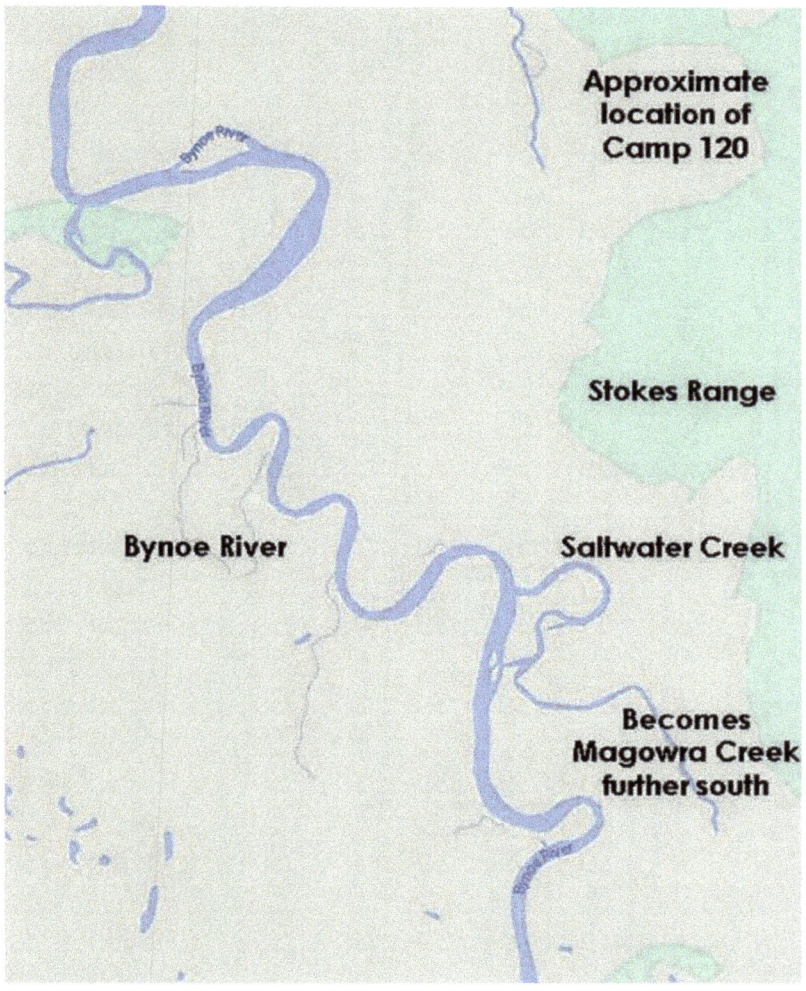

Choosing a Path

Travelling along the Norman River by boat is one way to access the northeastern area above the Stokes Range between two of its tributaries, the locally named Four- and Six-Mile creeks. The official name for Six-Mile Creek is the Russell. The easterly section of Russell Creek is just north of the northern end of the Stokes Range.

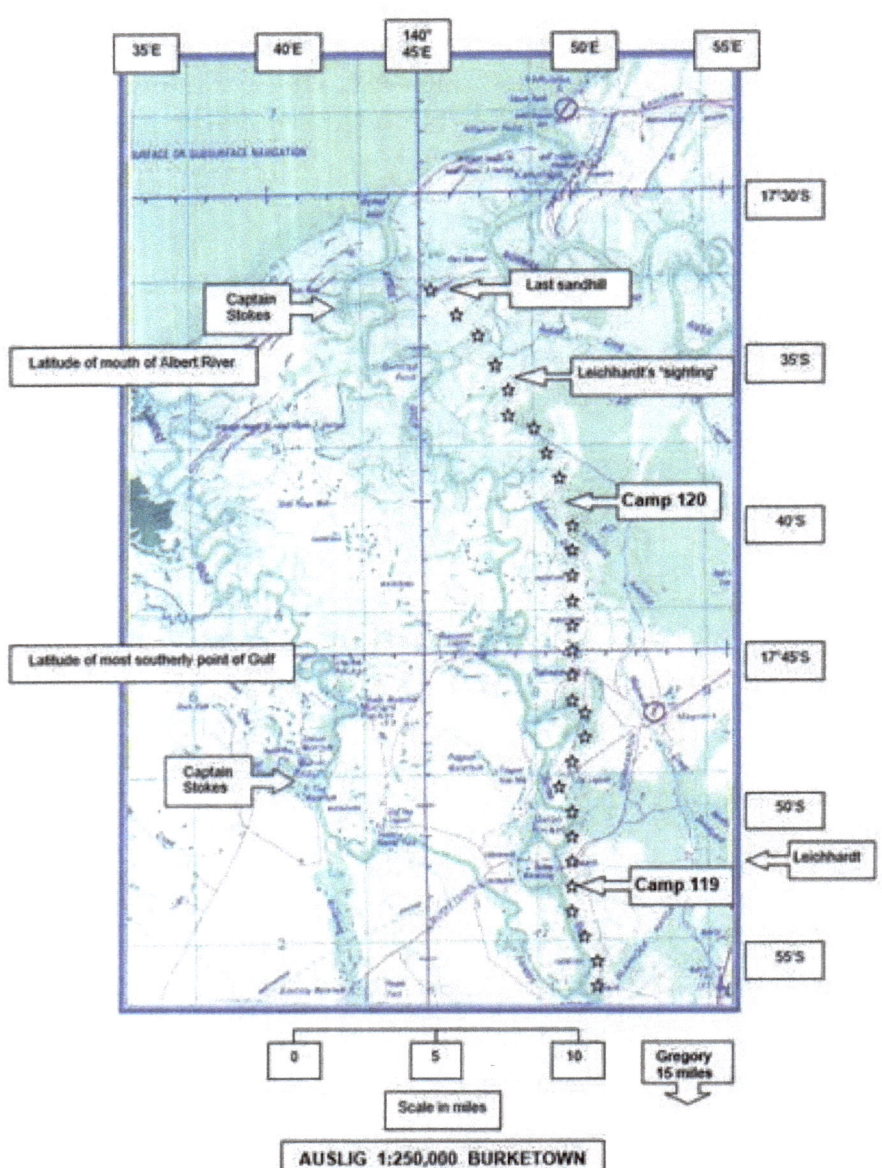

This creek's change in direction happens to be within half a mile of Burke and Wills' most probable route on their last day north. But we did not gain any clues at that point, which is many miles north of where we eventually located Camp 120. (See top right-hand corner of the part of AUSLIG map 1:250 000 shown left.) We chose not to access the area from the Norman River, believing that we could reach it more easily from Saltwater Creek.

A boat can provide western access into the Bynoe River and then into Saltwater Creek, but that boat must be adequately equipped. The round trip from Karumba can be over seventy nautical miles. The magnitude of just this part of the trip would discourage most people. Therefore, we needed a reasonably-sized and well fitted-out craft to ensure a safe journey.

Entering the Bynoe River

The tides in the Bynoe River and Saltwater Creek are about two and a half hours later than in Karumba and, for safety reasons, we did not navigate any creeks or upper reaches on an ebbing or low tide. Instead, we set out only during high tide cycles, which occurred every fortnight in the months of the year when we were there, and peaked at over three metres.

The next leg of the journey, the Bynoe River, can be accessed on such tides from Karumba. We took our craft heading south-southwest from the sand island near the Norman River shipping channel to a point about two nautical miles seaward in line with the Bynoe River. Then we headed into the river mouth on a south-southeast course.

Two submerged Second World War moorings for Catalina flying boats lurk in the muddy waters just before the mouth of the river and could cause disaster on certain tides. On the way out of the Bynoe, if we were to follow the same route on a much lower tide, our boat could go aground. We would instead have to follow the channel. Groundings could result in staying put for over a week on a falling tide cycle. This happened to one navigator in 1997 a few miles east of the Norman River during an attempted night voyage. However, his luck was in. He was only about two hundred yards offshore, right opposite the bar of the Sunset Tavern at Karumba Point, which was well within wading distance. A very handy spot for keeping an eye on the situation.

The details of the Bynoe channel entrance are not shown on any Nautical Charts and cannot be determined readily on-site because of zero water visibility due to suspended mud particles. I was fortunate enough to have an AUSLIG air photo from 1965 showing clear water in the channel, so I was able to produce a chart (see below) with survey control taken from that AUSLIG sheet. This gave me the appropriate latitude and longitudes, and scale.

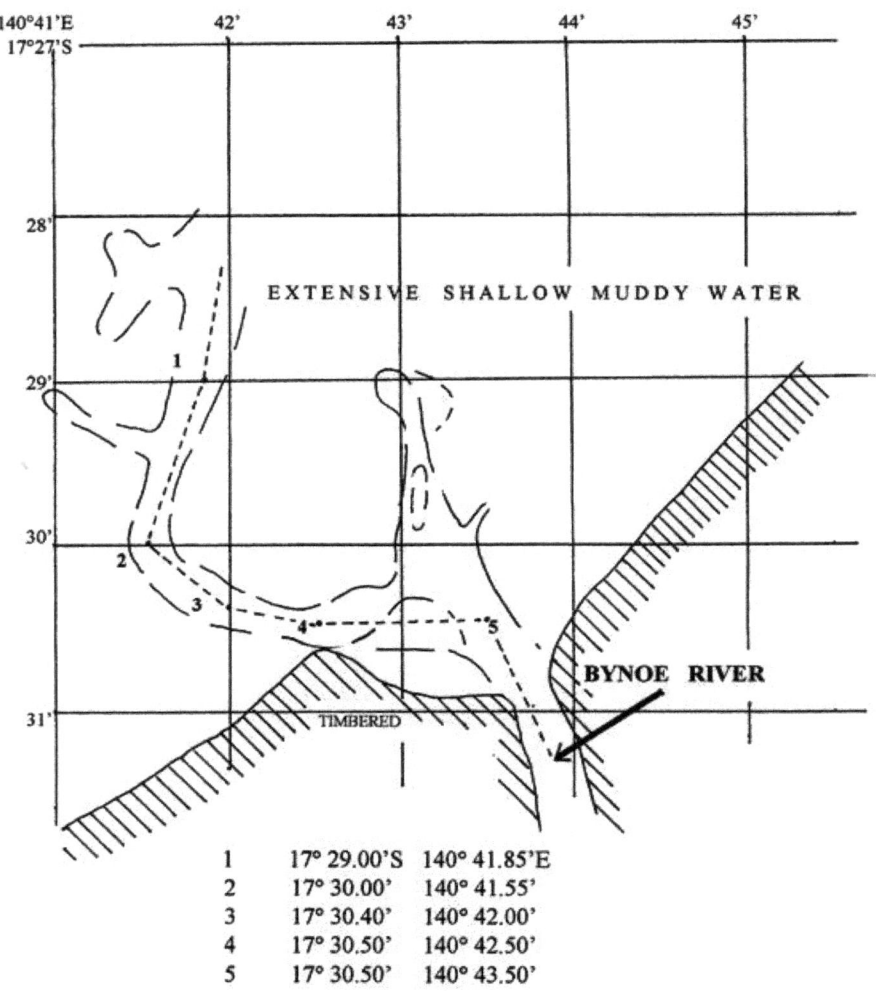

1	17° 29.00'S	140° 41.85'E
2	17° 30.00'	140° 41.55'
3	17° 30.40'	140° 42.00'
4	17° 30.50'	140° 42.50'
5	17° 30.50'	140° 43.50'

CHART OF BYNOE RIVER ENTRANCE

Produced from AUSLIG 1965 air photograph BURKETOWN, CAB 4015 number 3343
Plus on-site adaptation near point 2 as a result of a channel change.
Air photograph control from AUSLIG 1:100000 MAGOWRA.

A GPS is essential on this trip as there are no channel markers. Caution is still required as changes can occur year to year. Our first attempt to use the new chart was successful.

We surprised some professional fishermen early one morning with our high-speed entrance through the mouth of the Bynoe River.

One highlight of our explorations by boat happened when we were heading up the Bynoe at speed. We heard a thump as the propeller hit something and, looking back, saw a flash of white. Turning around, we found a large barramundi floating belly up. This looked like dinner to us, so we picked it up and found it was tagged. By law, all tags had to be returned to the Fisheries Department in Karumba.

When we arrived in Karumba to hand in the tag, the Fisheries Officer gave us a serious look. He then remarked that it had better not be one that had been stolen from their breeding tanks a few days before. Fortunately for us, it turned out to be a fish that had been tagged and released a year earlier from the Karumba facility at the mouth of the Norman River. It had travelled a considerable distance to finish up in the Bynoe River. Dinner that evening was very much enjoyed.

We were fond of telling everyone that we caught it on a twelve-inch spinner, alias the propeller of our boat.

Suitable tide cycles are severely restricted and opportunities for access are further restricted by the aftermath of the Wet. Later in the year, the tide cycles give high tides at night so the months of September to December are unsuitable as are January and February for the same reason.

To navigate to the vicinity of Camp 120 from Saltwater Creek, we had to cross, on foot, a small billabong-type creek just west of Camp 120 at the foot of the Stokes Range. This was only possible at about the end of April in 1997 and mid-July in 1998. Any earlier attempts could have seen a very muddy experience, and all without a successful crossing. Locating the best crossing place on the billabong is easy with a simple trick: follow the cattle tracks. A successful crossing is also entirely dependent on the seasons. The tropical area sees very wet summers and dry winters.

Using a boat in these waters can be hazardous. I always recommend safety precautions, including advising someone reliable of your proposed route and what time you intend to return.

Submerged logs can be one of several problems. One of the victims of this type of accident was Captain Stokes, Commanding Officer of the *Beagle* on his trip up the adjacent Flinders River in the 1840s. He records: -

Some grassy islets were scattered here and there, reposing in emerald verdure on the surface of the stream, which was reverting under the influence of the tide, towards its source, and now hurried the boat so rapidly through a narrow channel between the west side of a large island and a low line of earthy cliffs, as to carry her foul of a submerged tree and half fill and almost capsize her. To ascertain the extent of the damage, we landed on a small sandy beach. [i]

This is not a bright prospect in crocodile-infested water. I was also concerned about changing a damaged propeller — not an easy task in any boat, even with an outboard motor where the propeller can be raised above the water level.

Speaking of crocodiles.
Once, when we were walking around a waterhole, I (the long-suffering wife) happened to spot a gaggle of Burdekin ducks on the other side of the water. I was carrying my camera and watched with interest as the birds dithered about in a group having a discussion before waddling along the edge of the waterhole then strangely veering away for a few steps before turning back down to the water's edge.
I wondered what on earth they were doing.
When we returned to camp and I downloaded the photos onto my computer, I realised exactly what they were doing (see next page): avoiding the crocodile, of course.

CHAPTER 5: THE GULF COUNTRY

"May we pass, Sir"

"Passing now, Sir"

"Thank you, Sir"

Uncovering the Land's Secrets

The extremely flat nature of this area helped to guard its secrets. At one place that Burke and Wills visited while out north from Camp 120, distant views were hindered by scrub and small trees. This frustrated my research as I continually asked myself why they did not go to higher ground for a view. Surely, they knew such an elementary tactic of best bush practice?

The answer was simple once I visited the site. They could not see any high ground due to the flat nature of the country with its low, light scrub. I then realised that Frederick Walker's height estimates of the Stokes Range were exaggerated due to the difficulty in determining what was level in the low flats between the small rises east of the Bynoe. Walker also had the height advantage of being on horseback. I pursued a multitude of alternatives on individually produced maps, but these all diverted me hopelessly off track.

In the past, detailed maps were not available to researchers, but recently they have become more readily obtainable. Progress is such that I could get them from AUSLIG on CD-ROM and upload them onto a laptop computer. Air photos are even more important; however, they are only available if you know about them. While you could purchase air photos on order, they are not usually available over the counter, with the exception of high-demand images such as around capital cities.

The way to take full advantage of air photos is with a stereoscope. That is a specialist piece of equipment used by a few surveyors and some geologists. I found it to be of great benefit. The stereoscope can combine the overlapped section of two air photos. The view appears as a three-dimensional image and highlights features that are not obvious on a single photograph. This piece of equipment was of major importance in my investigation because it gave the first clue to the potential location of Camp 120. A pocket stereoscope proved inadequate for the task due to the flat nature of the country. Instead, I had to use a larger desk top model with a wider eye base (due to the inclusion of mirrors), as it further magnified the differences in the height of the land.

Another obstacle to my quest was time. I doubted that the mystery would be solved in a day or so. Therefore, any search had to be a serious undertaking. I allowed three months on-site on the project for the first season and was prepared to spend similar amounts of time there in subsequent years, if necessary. The off-site research required an even greater time commitment, which is reflected in the number of source materials quoted. Extracting clues found on- and off-site proved to be a slow process.

CHAPTER 5: THE GULF COUNTRY

Example of a stereoscope

Crocodiles are the unofficial guardians of the site. Many large crocodiles roam the area and they are not as timid as those in more frequented areas. However, they are not as plentiful as those shown in Frank Clune's photo fronting page 145 in his book *DIG* of 1935. Wild pigs also occur intermittently in the area and can be more dangerous.

While riding through the bush on our 4WD bike, we startled a wild boar that had been sleeping. We were almost upon it as it started to rise to its feet, and we had no space or time to turn the bike around and beat a retreat. David stood up with the rifle that was always carried across the front of the bike for easy access. Realising he had forgotten to bring his earplugs, I hastily inserted mine, stood up behind him and reached up to put my fingers in his ears while he despatched the boar. A pity no-one was there to take a photo of little me behind big, tall David with my fingers in his ears.

The area has its usual share of snakes and some of these are quite large.

One snake incident involved the long-suffering wife taking a shower in the bush.

We used to carry a bush shower kit, which included a black plastic bag that was filled with water and left on the bonnet of the truck. By the end of the day, the water was the perfect temperature for showering.

There I was, standing in a dish with the bag hanging over a branch, having a wonderful shower when I spotted a large snake strolling down the nearby track. It must have smelled the water because it lifted its head and turned towards me. I screamed for David who emerged dressed ready for his shower. He quickly assessed the situation, grabbed the rifle and his earmuffs, and despatched the snake in short order.

Unfortunately, I was not quick enough to grab my camera and snap David, wearing only little black jocks (underpants) and red earmuffs.

Access to the area around Camp 120 will probably never change and it will always be remote with a significant element of danger. The cycle of tides and the drying process after the wet season severely restrict access by foot or by boat. The Century Zinc pipeline, constructed in 1998 with a track along its length, is well south of the Camp 120 area and therefore of little use.

CHAPTER 6
THROUGH NORTH QUEENSLAND

Having set the scene of our mystery, it is worth looking at the travels of the Burke and Wills' Expedition leading up to Camp 119.

The 1861 crossing of the watershed range either side of Camp 100 proved to be dangerous, particularly for the camels. Having successfully navigated the crossing, the Burke and Wills Expedition then followed the route down the river system through the hills west of Cloncurry. This was the only practical way to make northern progress due to ground conditions, topography and assured water each night. The banks of the Corella were beautiful in this area and may have been the best aspect of the whole trip for camps and pleasant travel. A typical Corella riverside scene is shown below.

The Corella River, near Camp 101 — paradise compared with previous camps

By following the river, their route took them up to 50' E (50 minutes of longitude east). However, Wills did not record any concern. Why not? Prior to the crossing Wills mentioned several times that they carried a large quantity of water each day to guard against dry overnight camps.

Some of his comments were: -

> Sunday, 30th December. ...taking a ten days' supply of water, as there were ranges visible to the north, which had the appearance of being stony.
>
> Tuesday, 8th January 1861. Started at a quarter past five A.M. with a load of water, determined to be independent of all creeks and watercourses.
>
> Thursday, 10th January 1861. At twenty minutes past five A.M., we left our camp with a full supply of water, determined to risk no reverses, and to make a good march. [i]

He also made comments on other occasions as to why they did not carry large quantities of water. No mention of this practice was made after crossing the range. They also made no note of having to turn back at any stage because of lack of water. This shows that their daily starts with camels were extremely efficient. Were these factors good luck or good management? I believe it was the latter.

Wills records the following about the Corella (the river he called the Cloncurry): -

> After running between three or four miles in this manner, it took a turn to the west, at which point there is a fine waterhole, and then assumed its original character. Below this we found water in several places, but it all seemed to be either from surface drainage or from springs in the sand. The land in the vicinity of the creek appears to have received plenty of rain, the vegetation everywhere green and fresh; but there is no appearance of the creek having flowed in this part of the channel for a considerable period. [ii]

Since then, scientists have credited the year 1861 as being an exceptionally wet year in south west Queensland. Based on this evidence and Wills' notes I do not believe any claims that it was just as wet further north.

Only on their return journey south did they experience delays due to rain.

Navigating with True North, Latitude & Longitude

Past researchers have criticised the Burke and Wills Expedition for being off course up to a hundred miles east due to bad navigation. Some of them suggest that it was possibly due to a mistake in travelling Magnetic North.[iii] Such a suggestion is insulting to a professional navigator, then or now. Wills' own written notes record at one point: -

> As far as we could see in the distance, and bearing due north, was a large range, having somewhat the outline of a granite mountain. The east end of this range just comes up to the magnetic north. [iv]

This comment was made southwest of Cloncurry when the ranges were starting to deflect the Expedition's route eastward. It shows that he was most certainly aware of the existence of and the difference between Magnetic and True North in his calculations, as covered previously.

Peter Latemore explains the difference between Magnetic and True North: -

> So you are standing on the site with your trusty compass which is pointing North… but is it? Your compass is showing you the direction of Magnetic North not True North. What is the difference and do we care?

> Because the Earth is a great big magnet, your compass (also a magnet) points to Magnetic North which is somewhere in the wilds of the Canadian Arctic and is moving a very small amount from year to year.

> True North indicates the point at the "top" of the Earth where the rotational axis emerges, i.e. the North Pole. It is in the Arctic Ocean and is a fixed point.

Because Magnetic North is a constantly moving point, it was necessary for Wills to take regular position fixes by observing the heavens to ensure that they were travelling in the correct direction.

Part of the night sky as it might have been seen by Wills

Latitude and longitude fixes were taken about every three days through the Camps 90–99, just south of the range crossing. When inspecting the area on the ground, I noticed the long vistas that would have been available to the explorers. This allowed them to easily track their longitude position by compass and estimation, thereby maximising the efficiency of their travel time. Longitude observations are more complex and time consuming than latitudes. To avoid multiple lengthy calculations, the party restricted direction changes to one or two a day.

Additionally, many people may underestimate navigators' ability to keep track of direction on sunny days. A good navigator is also aware of the angle of their shadow.

Challenges of the Terrain

To give some idea of the remoteness of the area, we were once camped on the boundary between two stations about eighty kilometres from the nearest homestead. The driver of the grader who was grading the fence line was seriously surprised to come upon us in such a remote location and very happy to have a cup of tea and a good chat.

Near Camp 94 Wills records: -

> having crossed the creek, our course was due north as before, until at about six miles, we came in sight of the range ahead, when we took a north-half east direction for the purpose of clearing the eastern front of it. [v]

This was a repetition of a problem they had experienced two days before. This northerly obstruction continued to Camp 99 and is clearly visible on the AUSLIG sheet DUCHESS. Due to the pale colouring of the contours, I found a soft pencil best to highlight the crest of each ridge on my map so that I could determine high points. The ridges, which run up to the Standish Ranges to the west, are approximately six miles apart and head in a northwesterly direction, separated by parallel creeks. The Expedition party kept their route as low as practical, bearing in mind that they were trying to follow the 140° longitude. After firsthand observation of the route, I was duly impressed by their decision to avoid the high points and thus give maximum consideration to their camels. As "new chums" they had learnt a lot about managing their animals.

At about Camp 99, or in the afternoon prior to it, the Expedition party would have been genuinely concerned that the ranges were quickly closing in on them. They had two choices. One was to continue their current north-easterly course and deflect even further to the east, pushing them considerably off course. The second choice was to turn northwest and accept the challenge of scaling the range. The AUSLIG sheet DUCHESS shows names used by Wills in his notes for many peaks but associates these names with peaks different to the ones named officially by Burke and Wills. This adds confusion and hinders the task of identifying their actual route using this map.

Up until Camp 92 they had generally followed longitude 140° as calculated by them, at about 139° 56' in today's terms (4' west at Camp 85, 7' west at Camp 86). This calculation was near to the average between the Albert River and the Flinders River as shown on Ludwig Leichhardt's map of 1845. It is not correct to compare the actual distances between the river mouths or to use today's maps. Leichhardt's is the only map relevant to understanding their situation as it was the only land map that was available to Wills at that time.

McKinlay, who led one of the four Burke and Wills relief expeditions in mid-1861, did not aim at the river mouth. He was looking for Augustus Gregory's[vi] route of 1854 with its known relationship to the river, since the difficulties of following the Albert

River were well documented at that time. The deflection, caused by the range, was known to Wills. The Burke and Wills Expedition party instead travelled well up the western water catchment area, and the river that formed the basis of the catchment area was turning to the northeast. This is shown diagrammatically on the tracing of Wills' plan. Travelling high up the catchment area also had the disadvantage of reducing their chances of finding water. Obviously, the best opportunity to find water is at the lowest point in the catchment, along the main river system. At this stage it seems that they were not prepared to move east, down into the lower reaches of the water catchment area that they were traversing, to improve their access to water.

From the AUSLIG map, it appears the route between Camps 96 and 97 would have been the most difficult and dangerous to date for the camels. At Camp 97 Burke recorded: -

> Still on the ranges; the camels sweating profusely from fear. [vii]

At Camp 99 Burke made a significant decision and recorded it in his notebook. For Burke, this was a rare occurrence and is one of the very few surviving notes he recorded for the whole journey. He clearly deemed it important to explain their actions. It states: -

> I determined today to go straight at the ranges, and so far the experiment has succeeded well. The poor camels sweating and groaning but we gave them a hot bath in Turners Creek, which seemed to relieve them very much. At last through, the camels bloody, sweaty & groaning. [viii]

We once joined a group of grey nomads (retirees touring by caravan around the country) for a day's camel ride from Karumba to explore the nearby bush. David's camel, Lily, walked behind mine and I remember she had the prettiest long eyelashes. However, she objected strenuously to carrying him because, not only was he quite heavy, but she had to carry the water also. Hence, she spent a lot of time sitting down.

If you have ever seen a camel sit down, you will know that the front end goes down first followed by the back end. Because their legs are long, the rider is first nearly tipped over the head and then nearly tipped over backwards giving the spine a severe tweak in the process.

In addition to that challenge, the gait of a camel is awkward and the saddles we were using were not the most comfortable. At the end of the day, the men in the group announced that there would be no conjugal relations for at least a week.

Camp 100 was in what they named Kings Gap near the top of the saddle that separates the watershed of the Corella and Cloncurry rivers (the camp would have been located below the saddle on a small creek to enable access to water). Wills recorded it as latitude 20° 54' 30", longitude 140° 13'. With current mapping I believe that it could be the saddle whose longitude is 140° 06', i.e., 7' west of Wills' calculations, consistent with his other observations.

Wills describes this crossing of the range as "the most dangerous part of the journey". [ix] The decision to take the route anyway demonstrates that Wills was keeping Burke informed of the longitude shift and its effect on their coastal objective. The AUSLIG map confirms that the decision to cross the ranges was the best option. Apart from another crossing option two miles further west, it was perhaps the only crossing point available to them. This shows that they were making considered and deliberate decisions. In fact, even with infinitely more information and today's more accurate equipment, they could not have made a better decision.

CHAPTER 7
TECHNOLOGY OF THE TIMES

As my research progressed, I found that current technology could add a completely new dimension to Wills' work. He could easily determine fairly accurate latitudes, given reasonable observing conditions. Determining longitudes was more difficult as they required precise time, which meant having an accurate pocket chronometer. Ships had access to box chronometers, but surveyors and explorers used pocket chronometers[i] that required careful and ritual attention.

Wills had three chronometers: his most accurate, a backup and a general work one. The two best chronometers were by watch and chronometer maker Murray, SN 5094 and 5243. The other was by Russell.[ii] The one Wills still had with him when he died eventually went to his nephew who, in 1937, was about seventy years old and lived in Narrandera.[iii]

An old chronometer

CHAPTER 7: TECHNOLOGY OF THE TIMES

Matthew Flinders used six chronometers, two large and four small. [iv] Ludwig Leichhardt had only one.[v] This highlights Wills' attention to detail. Poor longitudes have been the curse of navigators for centuries and have been the cause of many major sea catastrophes. Accuracy improved in 1760 when English carpenter and clockmaker John Harrison invented the modern timekeeper, a larger and much more accurate version of a pocket watch, for use at sea. [vi] He won a prize of a remarkable, for those times, 20 thousand pounds. The Board of Longitude sponsored the prize to expedite research for more reliable ways to determine longitude following a maritime disaster in which most of the English Navy fleet foundered on the Scilly Islands off southwest England.

When telephone connections were made around the world, after Burke and Wills' time, it became easier to know the correct time at different places in the world. The advent of radio time signals and specialist precision theodolites in the 1950s also added to and improved navigational accuracy. More recently, satellite navigation and finally GPS have enabled further improvements. We can now accurately record latitude and longitude on a pocket GPS within thirty seconds, a degree of accuracy undreamed of by early explorers or navigators.

Early explorers Flinders and Stokes continually expressed concern about the accuracy of their longitudes. This was despite both having infinitely more resources of personnel and of time for observations than any land-based explorer.

John Lort Stokes explored the northern coast of Australia in *HMS Beagle*. In 1840, while surveying Port Essington, the first settlement in the north prior to Darwin, Stokes recorded the following while observing for latitudes, much easier than observing for longitudes: -

> nearly a hundred observations with the sun and stars were made for latitude, the mean result being 11° 22' 21", which strange to say, was nearly 15 seconds greater than Captain Stanley and Mr. Tyers's determination: this difference to me was quite unaccountable, as the instruments used in the Beagle were before and subsequently, satisfactorily tested at well determined places. The longitude being affected by the doubtful meridian distance between Sydney and Port Stephen, we can only give an approximate result. [vii]

Regarding his work Stokes also stated: -

> The longitudes are generally given from meridians in Australia, as I much question whether any portion of the continent is accurately determined with reference to Greenwich. Sydney, Port Essington and Swan River, have been the meridians selected; [viii]

Stokes refers above to the meridians of longitude.

A chronometer does not keep perfect time but "should go at a uniform speed, so that its error changes uniformly".[ix] This may be either a gain or loss of time, much as modern clocks sometimes run slow or fast. The chronometer is calibrated (checked for accuracy) before departure and through previous practical use (one of Flinders' had been calibrated for fifteen months).[x] Navigators had to carry them the same way all the time and wind them at the same time each day. Variations of temperature and humidity also affected their operation and accuracy.[xi] This important daily ritual of winding at noon was always instilled into trainee navigators. Flinders documents a problem whereby he found that the timekeepers had stopped, "my assistant having forgotten to wind them up at noon... former accidents of the same kind".[xii]

And again: -

> No.520 had been accidentally let down in Blue-mud Bay, whence its longitude is not now noticed. [xiii]

Recovery from these disasters took additional time for Flinders, and Wills would not have wished for this type of delay on his dash for the Gulf. He records no such lapse in his notes. Burke and Wills planned their Expedition to be conducted over an extended period of time. Thus, they could not possibly have calibrated their chronometers sufficiently for the circumstances. Under normal circumstances they would have checked and re-calibrated the devices on return to Melbourne and Wills would have been able, as a result, to slightly adjust his longitudes. However, he could still not be exact due to temperature, transport and basic Melbourne longitude variations. Therefore, his longitude calculations would logically contain minor errors due to watch and other relevant issues, which were beyond his control.

Complicated stellar observations are another way to calculate the correct time. Wills probably lacked the time required to undertake these observations, except at camps where they stopped for two or more nights such as Coopers Creek on the way north. He also observed stellar information on the slow trip north prior to Coopers Creek at camps where they stayed for two nights. In Melbourne, Edwin Welch later received and reduced (re-calculated) these observations.[xiv]

These reductions provide evidence that Wills observed for latitude, longitude, watch error and magnetic variation of his compass. Latitudes and longitudes were observed as a set of six and the average taken. Wills also documented clear information and instructions regarding his artificial horizon and corrections to the sextant from calibrations including where that information was held in Melbourne.[xv] These observations provide a great deal of information about Wills that rebuts any theories or speculation that he was incompetent as a navigator. Nothing could be further from the truth.

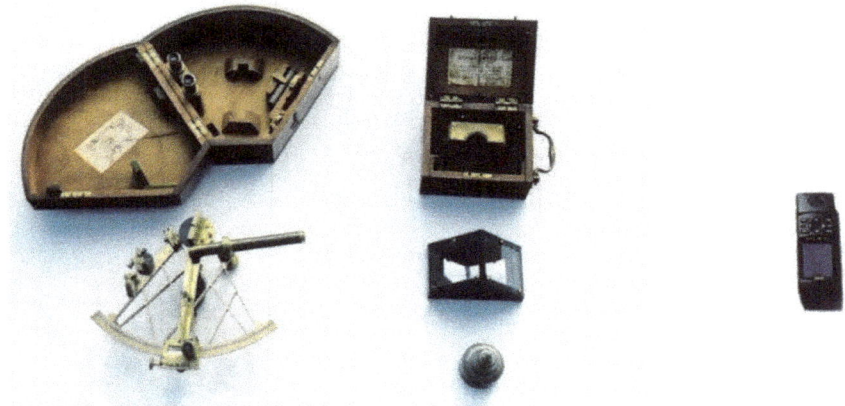

Examples of an early sextant and artificial horizon like the ones used by Wills; the 1990s handheld GPS on the right shows the approximate difference in size

The fact that Wills could observe and send all the raw information to Melbourne, to be reduced by another, tells us that he was very competent. He was fully aware of all the observations necessary to know exactly where he was, within the limits of his equipment. Wills would certainly have processed the observations himself and carried out the necessary calculations. These are the latitudes and longitudes that are shown in his plot (also called a plan) notes.

All that information would have been too voluminous and difficult to copy while in the field. It would have added bulk to the information being sent back to Melbourne, as well as adding bulk to equipment that was carried north for copying purposes. It would be unwise to deduce that Wills sent the raw information down only because he could not reduce and compute it himself. His calculations for magnetic variation show that he was aware of the difference between Magnetic and True North and therefore he would have corrected for the variation. It seems doubtful that he would go to all that trouble and then ignore the information after he computed it.

Even today, people visiting these remote parts of Australia find it challenging to send information and communicate with the world around them.

One year, about eighty kilometres south of our Normanton destination in the Gulf country, we came across an overturned 4WD vehicle and trailer on a gravel road. The husband-and-wife occupants had both been injured but the wife, who was a nurse, had managed to get herself out of the car. Her husband was still trapped. She assured us that their injuries were not life-threatening.

Another car had already stopped to offer help, but the two people clearly needed medical assistance. Fortunately, we carried with us a satellite phone because, apart from a flying doctor radio, it was the only way to communicate in such remote places. Not even standard mobile phones would work. We called our friends in Normanton who notified the local police with details of the accident. Within an hour, police and a medivac helicopter arrived. They extricated the husband and then took the couple to Mt Isa hospital. We stayed to help the police collect all their belongings, which were scattered along the road, before continuing our journey.

This incident demonstrated the need to carry a great deal of safety equipment and also to learn country driving skills.

Challenges for Past Navigators

Wills highlighted the time error caused by variations of the chronometer. The only errors he could not correct for were possible errors in the Nautical Almanac he carried, errors in the longitude calculations from Melbourne at the time of his departure and any errors in the existing maps and charts of the Gulf.

Melbourne's longitude at that time was incorrect and therefore affected the accuracy of Wills' observations. This can be seen clearly when Wills' observations are examined today. There was no telegraph connection at that time to enable greater accuracy.

Nautical Almanacs have been produced annually for hundreds of years and are available to this day. They contain information to aid navigators, particularly at sea, in celestial navigation using the positions of specific stars in relation to the globe that, once measured, can determine a position on the Earth. However, they did not record latitudes and longitudes for Australian Observatories until 1868.

CHAPTER 7: TECHNOLOGY OF THE TIMES

In addition, we know for certain that we can examine the development of Melbourne's longitude through recordings by the past Government Astronomer. To quote from the preamble of one of his reports: -

> The rapid increase in the maritime intercourse of the Australian Colony of Victoria which took place directly after the discovery of her rich and extensive gold-fields in 1851 and 1852 soon led to the pressing necessity of providing some authorised and trustworthy source from which correct local time could be obtained, for ascertaining the errors and rates of ships' chronometers, and a recognized establishment to which masters of vessels could refer with confidence for testing, adjusting, or safe custody of their nautical instruments generally. To meet this requirement the Colonial Government decided upon establishing an Observatory at Williamstown, and in July 1853, appointed Mr. R. L. J. Ellery to organize and permanently superintend it.

> On entering upon this task he found several preliminary arrangements already made; a time ball had been erected on Gellibrand's Point, some instruments ordered from England, a site for the Observatory selected…

A public time signal was commenced in August 1853, by dropping a ball on the Williamstown Flagstaff at one o'clock local time every day. This signal was watched from the Melbourne Flagstaff, about 4 1/2 miles distant, by the aid of a telescope, and a ball was dropped there also, as nearly as possible at the same instant as that at Williamstown…

The observations for obtaining true local time were at first made with the sextant, artificial horizon, and chronometer, the geographical position assumed being that given to Gellibrand's Point by Capt. Stokes of H.M.'s surveying ship Beagle, namely, lat. 37° 52' 52", long. 9h 39m 42secs. (144° 55' 30")…

A few months subsequently a 20-inch transit instrument and the works of a good astronomical clock were obtained and mounted in a small building erected for them…

The instruments ordered from England arrived in March 1854, consisting of a time ball and apparatus, a 25-inch transit instrument, and a very superior astronomical clock by Frodsham…

Until the middle of 1858 the work of the observatory had been for the most part confined to observations for the regulation of time, observations of the moon and the moon-culminating stars for the determination of the longitude, and the zenith distances of known stars with the altazimuth with a view to the determination of latitude. [xvi]

From June 1860 (about the time Burke and Wills headed north) the observatory commenced a programme to update its longitude. This continued until February 1862 when the results were collated. The new value for the longitude of Melbourne was 144° 54' 42", i.e., 48" further west than the information available to Wills. The change in value would affect all his longitude calculations by the same amount since it affected the time calibration of his chronometers. The new value also shows that Stokes' longitude work from twenty years earlier only needed upgrading by 45" longitude. This was an outstanding initial observation by Stokes considering that he used a sextant, while the observatory used much larger fixed instruments and observed over an extended period in parallel with the Cape of Good Hope and Greenwich.

I had thought this minor variation and characteristic of chronometers would be of interest only to navigators. But a person involved in pigeon racing once told me about certain practices of some unscrupulous pigeon racers. Some racers had discovered that their racing chronometers could be made to run fast by shaking them. This loophole has now been overcome by equipping the instrument with a meter that measures vibration — and if it shows a figure higher than four, the pigeon racer is disqualified.

They have also found that the chronometer slows if kept under refrigeration, only being removed for the check in. Pigeon racers have one hour fifty-five minutes after the race to arrive at the check in, therefore sometimes when they arrived the unit was still frosted. Navigators' chronometers have not had a similar temperature problem since the 1700s when temperature compensation was introduced, although that feature increased the cost of the unit.

Other forms of technology available today include the AUSLIG map and air photography. (See image on next page.) Burke and Wills followed the watercourses from Camp 101 on the Corella River down through the Dugal, Cloncurry, Flinders, Bynoe and Little Bynoe. That established a datum based on the river line to determine longitude at the riverside campsites which, according to today's maps, was very accurate. Using the equipment he had, and under the circumstances of the time, Wills passed all reasonable accuracy tests.

Wills' Records

Wills set out from a campsite at Coopers Creek, travelled halfway across Australia and then navigated the surviving Expedition members back to the same initial site without hesitation or delay. The final section of the return journey to Coopers Creek's camp was travelled after dark — possibly without a sextant for the last few days of the journey. This represents a combination of excellent navigation skills and bushcraft skills. The work was certainly was not the result of an incompetent navigator.

I plotted and recorded twenty consecutive northern camps using Wills' calculated positions where they abutted a creek or river that could be readily identified. Spanning 207 miles, eighteen of the camps were east of their actual location and two were to the west. Wills notes for these show remarkable consistency, and minor errors are likely due to the Melbourne datum, watch or Almanac error.

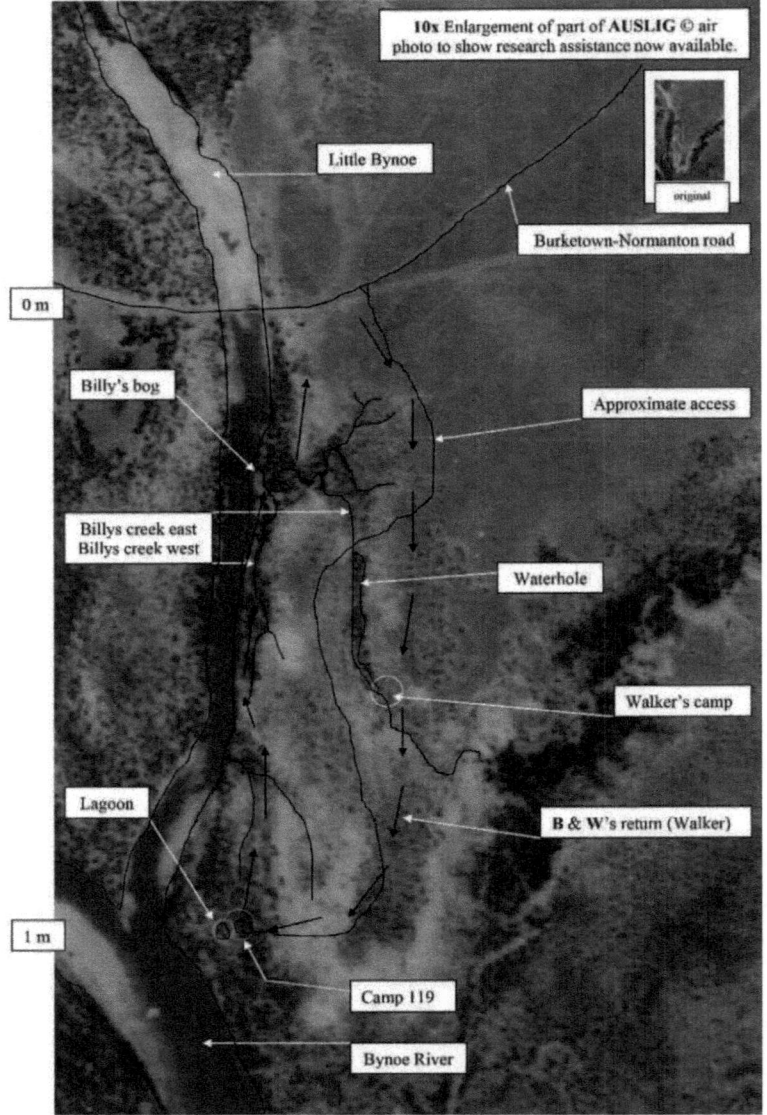

Consecutive camp observations in the northern area after they crossed the range highlights how dedicated Wills was and interested in calculating their daily position. His observations even include longitudes, which required complex calculations. These latitudes and longitudes can be seen on a tracing made of Wills' original northern section of his survey. This is held in the Australian Manuscript Collection, Latrobe Library, State Library of Victoria headed "Map of Burke And Wills Route copied from the map prepared by Mr. Wills" (original lost shortly after the copy was made when the Expedition's equipment returned to Melbourne).

My plotting verifies that the tracing is a faithful copy of the original with possibly two clerical errors in tracings at Camps 95 and 99. Further south is a definite 10° clerical error at Camp 72 and possible 20' error at Camp 74. I make no claim that this is a complete error list. The errors on the plots could have been Wills' as he transferred them from his calculations, or it could have been by the tracer in Melbourne. However, as Wills was working with the information and depending on them to determine their location and direction of travel, I doubt that they were his errors. The plot shows Camp 72 at latitude 37° 02', while Melbourne's latitude is 37° 50'. Only a tracer in Melbourne could have made the 10° error by accidentally introducing the Melbourne figure. But Wills would have certainly noticed such an error on his plot.

How am I confident in this conclusion? Let's return to our gossamer globe. The 10° latitude represents the following error.

10° = 10 x 60' = 600' = 600 nautical miles = 690 statute miles = 1110 kilometres.

In rough figures this error claims the Expedition party travelled from the latitude of Coopers Creek to the latitude of Melbourne overnight. No doubt the party would have gladly welcomed such a miracle upon returning to the DIG tree at Coopers Creek after their long and arduous journey south. But fate was not to be so kind to them.

The other plot errors, although less than this 10° example, may explain the inaccurate naming of features south of Cloncurry on AUSLIG sheet DUCHESS. It also shows the latitudes and longitudes of the Government Astronomer in the same handwriting. None of the information on Wills' plots or in his notes could have been fabricated as it now stands the test of time and technology. When you compare Wills' calculations with the DIG tree at Camp 65, Wills is again to the east but only by 01' 30."[xvii] This small variation could be due to more time taken, more observations, less watch problems or just serendipity. The overall too-far-east error follows a virtually straight-line proportion all the way back to Melbourne, subject to a small plus or minus. Noticing and accounting for this type of error was not possible in those days but is easy with GPS technology and today's maps. To locate any of Burke and Wills' camps now from Wills original observations, we would search further west by a proportion of: -

0.80" longitude at Melbourne
1.50" longitude at Coopers Creek
4.20" longitude at Camp 109
plus or minus 2.00" longitude.

However, it might not be that simple. Minor checks south of Camp 100 suggest that the four-minute discrepancy may continue further south and there are problems with the first few camps north of Coopers Creek.

> The GPS fix for latitude at Camp 119 is 17° 52' 47"
> By Wills' observation and calculation 17° 53' 00"
> By Government Astronomer's recalculation 17° 53' 38"

This 13" difference of Wills' compares favourably with Stokes' 12" calculation after the one hundred observations at Port Essington previously mentioned. Wills certainly did not carry out one hundred observations — he would not have had the time.

Therefore, Wills' accuracy was, for the times, phenomenally good.

Past Criticism for Wills

The Government Astronomer re-computed several longitudes of Wills in the northern area but his recalculations for Camps 116 and 117 were obviously out by many miles. As the position of Government Astronomer carried much authority, the incorrect recalculations would have sullied Wills' reputation. This error likely added to the mystery of the Expedition and presented an unfounded basis for criticism by various historians. At the time of my research, I found no evidence that the Government Astronomer's work had been re-examined. History has now proved it wrong.

Augustus Gregory reviewed some exploration information of 1862 and strongly inferred that Wills' work was inaccurate. His comments were based on a report about how far a person had ridden on a horse over several days. To favour that kind of information against readings with a sextant is astounding. Current information now shows that Gregory's assumptions about Wills' return route were flawed and should not have been made.[xviii]

In 1888, Ernest Favenc wrote his review of one hundred years of Australian exploration. In this we find what appears to be a reflection of the views of that time. Views that have, despite new evidence, persisted to the present day in some quarters.

> they did not actually know their position on the Gulf, being strangely out in their reckoning; mistaking the river they were on for the Albert, over a hundred miles to the westward. [xix]

Favenc's criticism was inordinately harsh since Leichhardt's plan showed 95 miles and Stokes showed only 65 miles between the two rivers. Favenc surmised that Burke and Wills were aiming at the Albert River, a belief that seems to be common among many past theorists and even some current ones. Evidence shows Wills generally followed his calculation of longitude 140° on his journey north of Coopers Creek, subject to the time error mentioned previously, and subject to the availability of water and suitable terrain for camels. His field books clearly observe the extent of the variations east and west in their hunt for water. However, the same source shows that the hills conflict with their route north of Camp 92 and Wills' plot and recorded longitudes also show this problem as discussed later. Suttor on page 485 of *Australian Milestones* records: -

> they mistook the river they were on for the Albert, which is over 100 miles to the Westward. Not knowing their position, they were much out in their reckoning.

This statement is most certainly not correct. We have no evidence that they thought that it was the Albert; they named it the Cloncurry and they were aware of the Flinders River in the general area. Since they knew of the Flinders, they must have known of its relationship with the Albert further to the west. Not once did they claim it to be the Albert. They certainly knew where they were for all practical purposes.

Examining the Data

When comparing early explorers' accuracy in this northern area with the AUSLIG maps, Hydrographic Charts and GPS, we see the following variations: -

Flinders at Sweers Island	+8' (42 sets of observations)
Stokes at Sweers Island	+6' (unknown number of sets)
Leichhardt at the Norman	22' (1 set)
Wills at 119	+6.46' (1 set)
Wills at 117–119 average	+5' (3 sets)
Wills at 109 (average 20 camps)	+4.2' (20 sets)
Gregory, none available	?
McKinlay, none observed	?? (only used compass and timed travel)

Examining Flinders' forty-two observation results for Sweers Island shows that he observed them in six sessions of 9, 9, 6, 3, 9 and 6 sets.

The highest value of longitude was 140° 12' 44"
The lowest was 139° 21' 22"
The average adopted 139° 44' 52"[xx]
i.e. a spread of 51' 22"

These figures highlight the differences that can occur on the one site and prove that even experienced observers such as Flinders and his officers could vary significantly. It goes a long way towards explaining the plus or minus differences of that era. Flinders' exploration and observations occurred sixty years before Wills', so his results probably bore the penalty of evolving Nautical Almanac tables and, to a limited degree, the evolution of equipment including that of chronometers (although Flinders had access at that time to the modern chronometer). All explorers of that era suffered a penalty as their basic chronometer settings came from different datum around Australia. The Australian Observatories could not yet coordinate time signals, so they all differed by different amounts since their data was built up from multiple continuing local observations.

Flinders and Stokes are regarded as the leading early navigators in Australian history. They not only received supporting observations from fellow officers, but they also operated without the pressure of time limitations and physical stress such as Wills experienced. In addition, they could use several different and larger instruments. Stokes had at least three officers who could navigate and it would be fair to assume that they competed to produce the "best" result. Flinders used at least two observers. Considering that Wills navigated alone, in difficult and physically demanding circumstances, and with a pressing time and supply problem, he performed outstandingly.

Wills, a young but experienced surveyor, had by far the best results of the three — Flinders, Stokes and himself.

CHAPTER 8
PREVIOUS EXPLORERS

Having established that they knew where they were and were not, as many believe, hopelessly out in their reckonings — let us return to their journey north.

Within a day they were through the range to a river with reliable water. As they came across the top of the range from Camp 100, they would have been heading north-northwest. Directly in front of them, they would have seen what is now known as Mount Burstall (they named it Mount Nicholson) surrounded by rough and intimidating country. This area would be the location for the future Mary Kathleen uranium mine located on the northern side of the Cloncurry–Mount Isa road.

Continuing in a north-westerly direction to regain their route on the nominal 140° longitude was impractical. The hills to the north were now so intimidating as to make True North or northwest camel travel difficult, dangerous and most likely impossible. I can vouch from experience that it certainly is, and was, infinitely rougher than anything they had encountered to date.

On their way down the flat valley, they followed what is now known as Frank Creek. About mid-morning they named a hill on their right Mount Gowan and about mid-day named a small round high hill on their right that had an offset leaning appearance towards the east as Pisa Hill. This hill is half a mile from the south-eastern bank of the Corella River according to AUSLIG on sheet CLONCURRY, latitude 20° 49' 30", longitude 140° 05' 15". The name Pisa Hill was not on the list of prepared names in Burke's notebook; he only planned to name peaks in honour of friends and benefactors. Perhaps naming the peak after the Leaning Tower of Pisa reflects their humour, or more likely Wills'. They then travelled down to what is now named the Corella River, but they named it the Cloncurry River. A few miles before Camp 101, they named a large hill on their right Mount O'Shanassy.

The only logical option was to follow the river down until the country improved. The latest technology (satellite imagery) highlights their position and justifies their decision. They were not lost, they had not mistaken Magnetic North for True North, they knew their position each day and they were certainly not following the Albert River. They were up to date with previous explorations along the northern coast. How can we be confident this is true?

Firstly, Wills started to observe the latitude and longitude each day. Why? Perhaps, due to the lack of visibility and the meandering watercourse, it was the only way to keep track of their location, but I believe there was an additional reason.

As well as carrying a sextant, Wills carried a *Nautical Almanac*, mathematical tables and survey information from the charts of Flinders and Stokes for the coastline of the Gulf. He needed these to navigate accurately and know when to make a dash for the Gulf or even to know about the Albert and Flinders Rivers. Latitudes and longitudes, no matter how accurate, are useless without a base map giving relationships with other places.

Sources Available to Wills

Augustus Gregory and Ludwig Leichhardt were the only two land explorers in the northern area before Burke and Wills. Leichhardt had passed through the northern coastal area in July 1845. Two years later, he published his *Journal of an Overland Expedition in Australia, from Moreton Bay to Port Essington 1844–1845*. Gregory passed through the area around 1856. His paper on this exploration was read to the Royal Geographical Society in 1857. Burke and Wills' journey was well south of the tidal influence and the salt plains, dangers that he was aware of because of Leichhardt's publications.

Matthew Flinders and Captain John Lort Stokes were the only two mariners to have published relevant navigational data before the Burke and Wills Expedition. Flinders referred to a copy of Thevenot's chart of 1663 and included this with his published chart.[i] Stokes' charts are also known as Arrowsmith's charts when named after the draftsman Arrowsmith. (See next page for partial reproductions of both Flinders' and Stokes' work.)

Abel Tasman had also been through the area in the early 1600s, but Flinders' and Stokes' more recent and more accurate charts were of interest to Wills. Stokes' chart was by far the most important of the three because it was the most recent and the most detailed.

Gregory's information interested Wills only because it confirmed that he was on the Flinders River just south of the coastal flats. Gregory, after leaving the Albert River, had headed east-southeast to avoid the travel obstructions discovered by Leichhardt. Gregory knew of Leichhardt's creek and mangrove problems on the coastal plains and he wished to clear the lowlands, which he was successful in doing.

CHAPTER 8: PREVIOUS EXPLORERS

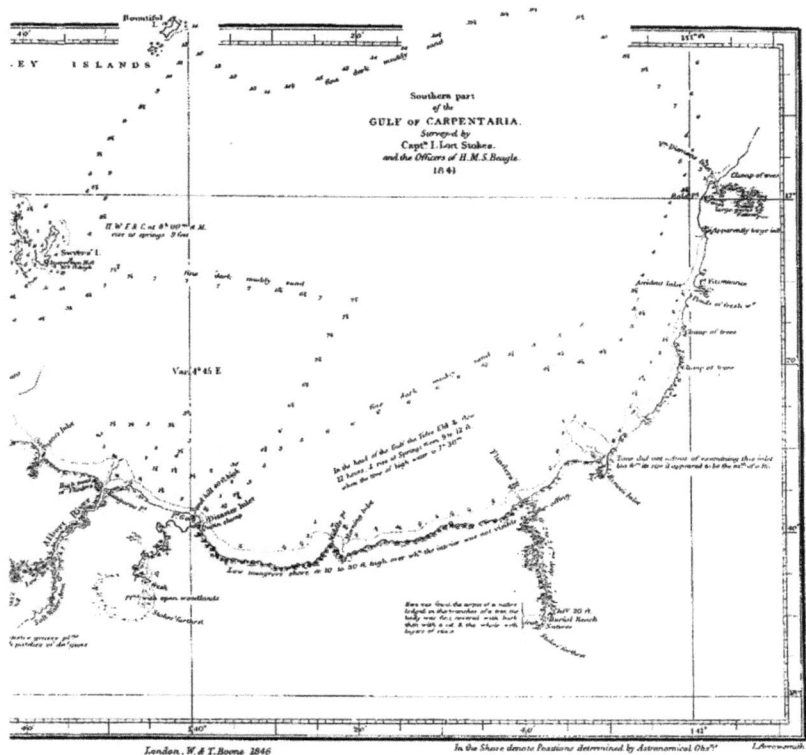

GULF CHARTS AVAILABLE TO BURKE & WILLS

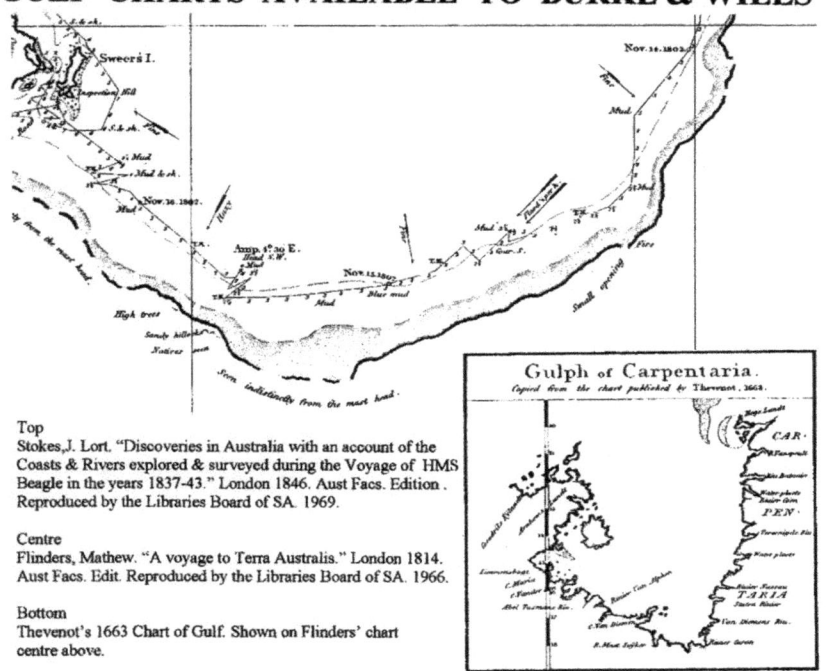

Top
Stokes, J. Lort. "Discoveries in Australia with an account of the Coasts & Rivers explored & surveyed during the Voyage of HMS Beagle in the years 1837-43." London 1846. Aust Facs. Edition. Reproduced by the Libraries Board of SA. 1969.

Centre
Flinders, Mathew. "A voyage to Terra Australis." London 1814. Aust Facs. Edit. Reproduced by the Libraries Board of SA. 1966.

Bottom
Thevenot's 1663 Chart of Gulf. Shown on Flinders' chart centre above.

The map attached to his paper for the Royal Geographical Society in 1857 (copy Rare Book Section, Mortlock Library of South Australia), confirmed his latitude on the Flinders River as being one mile north of where the present-day Burke Development Road crosses the Flinders River. Gregory's description of his journey two days before and one day after this crossing is brilliantly illustrated on the AUSLIG map including the description of two belts of north–south trees he encountered. This highlights the potential for more accurate historical research.[ii] It reveals possible errors recorded by the explorers when they compiled their reports later, perhaps from sketchy notes. For example, at this camp on the Flinders, Gregory states: -

> 10th September. 6:10am again found us in the saddle, and crossing to the right bank followed it to the south-southeast till 7:20, when it turned to the south-southwest, and changing our course to the east, passed through a fine grassy plain… [iii]

I was impressed by his description of the river's directions as it matches the AUSLIG map exactly. I speculated that he chose to follow the river south for general reconnaissance but when I walked up to the camp area, I found something completely unexpected. The location of his camp was on a section of the river that is wide and deep; there is no way he could have crossed at that point as he stated. More realistically, he must have followed the river south-southeast on the west bank until about 7:20am, then crossed on the rock bar where a road crosses today. Frederick Walker, who searched for the Burke and Wills party, raised many similar questions in his notes.

Leichhardt's map, in three parts, attached to his report was drawn by: -

> A Captain Perry (Deputy Surveyor General) is fully occupied in working out my maps systematically and neatly, and it is a pleasure to see how the country which I touched in my wanderings begins to stand out from the unknown and undescribed interior of Australia.
> [iv]

The maps, therefore, had more authenticity than Leichhardt himself could have foreseen. In 1964, the Libraries Board of South Australia produced a facsimile edition showing these three charts in all their detail. The more recent facsimile edition by Corkwood Press compacts the three charts into one and omits minor detail, which is essential to the study of Wills' navigation. We need two of the three Leichhardt charts showing the detail near the Flinders to understand what happened in Burke and Wills' situation and why.

The central sheet, more than any other documents, is the key to the Burke and Wills mystery in this northern area. It should be noted that Stokes' plan was published too late for Leichhardt to have taken a copy with him in the field.

Robert Logan Jack had considerable trouble trying to reconcile Leichhardt's plan and even gave a warning to future researchers "that way madness lies".[v] Later on the same page, he states that "Leichhardt's latitudes must be wrong.' I believe he is referring to longitudes, a simple and common clerical mistake, of which I have been guilty myself. In the vicinity of the Bynoe and Flinders Rivers, Leichhardt's latitude is only out by about two minutes. Remember that Leichhardt was travelling generally east–west, the same way that latitudes run. The description of madness applies more aptly to longitudes, which run north–south.

A Surveyor's Toolkit

To understand Wills' knowledge of his predecessors in the area we need to go back to his training as a surveyor. He commenced survey training in 1856 and amongst others he worked under the District Surveyor in Ballarat. He quickly graduated to leading his own survey party and was: -

> always in the bush marking out land for sale, or laying down unknown parts.[vi]

At that time, Victoria was undergoing a complete survey of the State to establish the lands title system with the land being divided into Counties, Hundreds, Parishes, Sections, and Townships with allotments.[vii] All the sections and allotments were for sale and these sales were funding the development of the State.[viii] A large team of surveyors worked on this as the amount of field work and calculations, without mechanical calculators or computers, was immense. The predominant dimension for rural work was the one square mile section. Surveyors, then or now, soon develop skills to estimate the distance they travel on foot while carrying out their survey work. Such skills used to find previous survey lines reduces field work and can speed up the overall survey time.

A surveyor engaged in any type of survey, and probably even more so on property surveys, must always "search" previous information in the area as everything he does builds on that previous knowledge. Therefore, from a surveyor's point of view, Wills certainly had a copy of previous exploration information about the gulf.

He would also have carried information regarding previous exploration in the Coopers Creek area and around Mount Hopeless. Charles Sturt and Edward John

Eyre were involved in those explorations and we can be certain Wills had that information; how else would the Expedition party know about an alternative way south from Coopers Creek? After they found no-one waiting for them on their return to Coopers Creek, they chose to head towards Mount Hopeless on the road to Adelaide. Later they had to retrace their steps due to lack of water. Sadly, while they were away, the relief party came back to Coopers Creek but, seeing no evidence that Burke and Wills had been there, left again.

Survey information often came in the form of a tracing, generally carried out by a draftsman or tracer and correct in every detail. This practice continued up until the recent advent of photocopiers. Access to plan information is not a resource only available via modern technology such as copiers.

Captain Stokes records that they were: -

> employing the time in completing our charts, sending home tracings of them. [ix]

Stokes records again much later: -

> and tracings, with other dispatches, being deposited with the Resident, to be forwarded to England. [x]

Stokes was only obeying the written orders of the Admiralty, which included in his orders the following: -

> and you will lose no opportunity, at those several places, of informing our secretary of the general outline of your proceedings, and transmitting traces of the surveys which you have effected, together with copies of your tide and other observations. You will likewise, by every safe opportunity, communicate to our Hydrographer detailed accounts of all your proceedings which relate to the surveys. [xi]

This was a slow process in those times, with information being left at ports of call to be carried back by other ships returning to their home base.

Burke, continuing this practice, left a copy of Wills' report with Brahe at Coopers Creek with instructions for its return to Melbourne in due course and wrote: -

> The accompanying tracing will show the course taken... [xii]

William Landsborough records another example of this practice from his journey of discovery in 1861 down to the Camooweal district in northwestern Queensland. This was one of four expeditions he led in search of the missing Burke and Wills

Expedition. Landsborough writes, referring to Lieutenant Woods, Chief Officer from the ship *HMCS Victoria* of the Victorian Navy, who drew up charts of the Albert River on the Gulf of Carpentaria where he started his journey south: -

> He made a beautiful tracing from the sketch I had made to show my route to the SW. [xiii]

This use of tracings to send information back had a twofold intention. It introduced new knowledge quickly and, more importantly, it safeguarded information in times when all sorts of disasters could befall it. We could understand Australian history better if Leichhardt had been able to send back a tracing from his last expedition during which his party disappeared.

If you use a computer these days, then you use the SAVE icon for the same reason (and backup all information, given the fickleness of computer technology).

Of all the navigators who preceded Burke and Wills, Flinders and Stokes had the most comprehensive information with them. Matthew Flinders in his preamble to Volume 1, *Voyage to Terra Australis*, devoted just under one hundred pages to list sources he had, which must have totalled a large volume of documents.

Wills' Use of Sources

When the Royal Commission held after the Burke and Wills Expedition questioned King, the only surviving member, they asked him about the locality of Camp 119: -

> Qu. 816 Who first made the discovery of reaching the sea, or did you all come upon it together; that is, reaching the salt water where the tide was?
>
> **King** Mr Wills knew it; he had told us two or three days before we reached the salt water that we were in the country that had been discovered by Mr Gregory and other previous explorers.
>
> Qu. 817 Some days before you got upon it he told you that?
>
> **King** Yes, and showed us on the chart the supposed place where Mr Gregory crossed this small creek.[xiv]

He used the words "this small creek". Does this indicate a lack of rain?

Gregory had camped on the west bank of the Flinders River, identified by him as such, at latitude 18° 08' 41" which is 2' 19" (2.5 miles) north of Camp 117. This camp is of course two days before Camp 119. His Flinders River identification confirms that Wills had a copy of Leichhardt's map and that Wills knew exactly where they were in relation to where previous explorers had been. His calculations were up to date and his plotting "on the chart" (as King stated) was also up to date.

This was certainly not the work of an incompetent.

Suttor, previously quoted; certainly not true: -

> Not knowing their position, they were much out in their reckoning.

The day before this they were following the Flinders in a northeasterly direction and they came to Camp 116 at the junction of the Saxby and Flinders Rivers. At this point they were at longitude 140° 51' and the river turned due north.

Leichhardt had described crossing a major river where the salt water ceased at latitude 17° 54' or 55', longitude 140° 45'[xv] — i.e., within six minutes longitude, which is seven miles due north.

If Wills had this information and, according to the above statement and his basic training as a surveyor, he must have, then it was possibly the same river. To confirm this, we need to examine evidence from after they travelled a further twenty-five miles down the river, i.e., further north.

When they reached Camp 119, Wills observed and computed the position of the campsite at latitude 17° 53', longitude 140° 56'. His calculations are a little over twelve miles east from Leichhardt's claimed position on the Flinders; could it be the same river?

Wills would have known that this difference could be caused by a small time error, either his or Leichhardt's or both. As Leichhardt reported that he only carried one chronometer, his ability to accurately observe for time corrections would have been suspect. In addition, Leichhardt calculated off the Brisbane datum while Wills worked off the Melbourne datum. Wills also knew that the observed longitudes of that time had little chance of agreeing exactly — in fact, they often differed by many minutes of longitude.

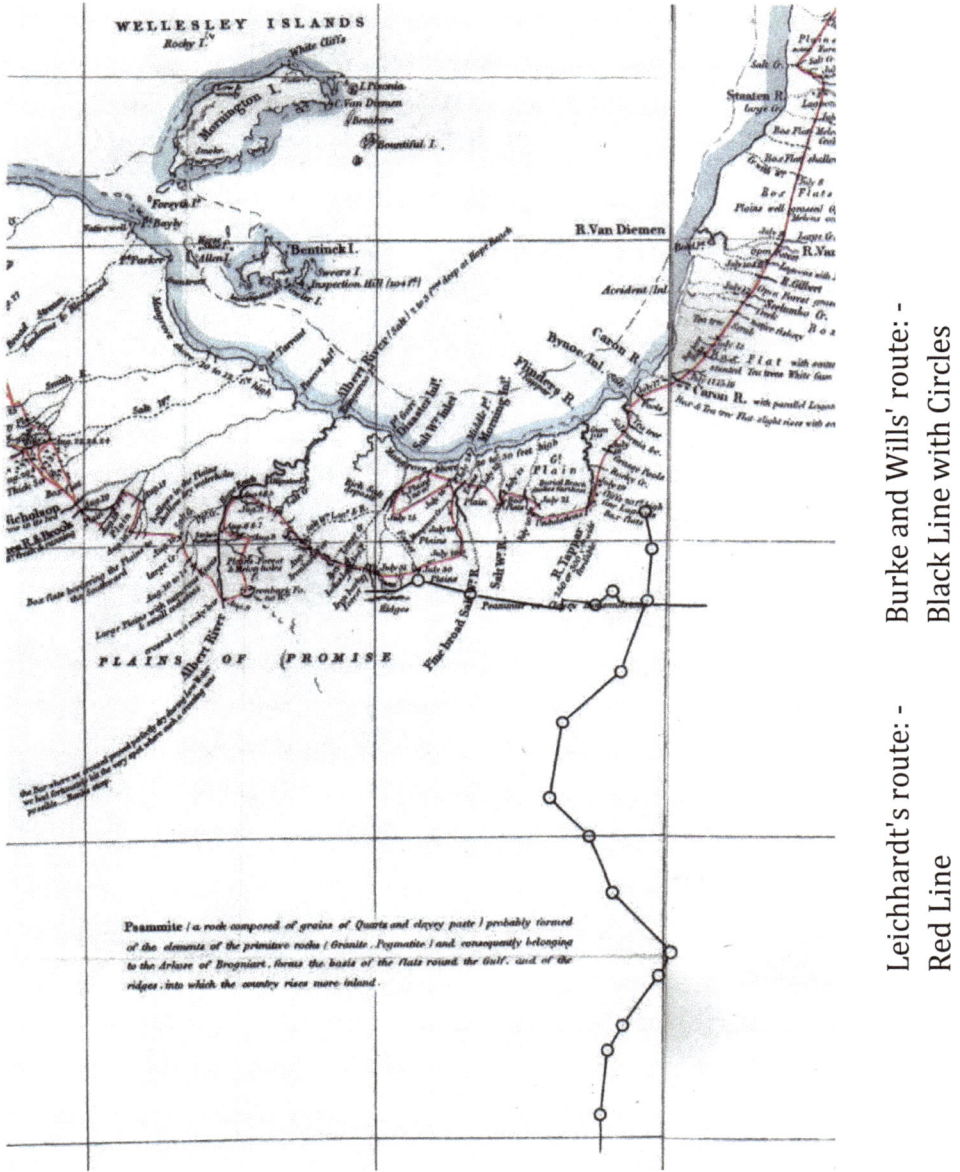

Wills knew of the fording opportunities near his camp that matched Leichhardt's description. Leichhardt's plan also showed no other river to the east of the Flinders River and Wills' position fix was to the east of Leichhardt's. Gregory also recorded no major river to the east, though he was slightly further south. Wills could come to no other conclusion but that they were on the Flinders River.

To suggest that Wills thought they were at the Albert River is completely wrong. From the time they followed the Corella, Wills' daily navigation observations for latitude and longitude showed that they were aware of this alternative access point to the Gulf. He knew within the observing accuracy of his instruments and mathematical tables where he was, and Leichhardt's detailed and recent plan confirmed his calculations. This is clear for us to see on his plan (see previous page).

Compounding Errors

Leichhardt recorded that, to the north of his river crossing, his forward scout Charley had sighted the sea on the 18th of July.[xvi] According to a plot of his day-to-day travels, this would have been at about latitude 17º 32'. This latitude is only 20 miles north of Camp 119. Wills had no way of knowing that this sea sighting was false. Even Leichhardt did not.

At this point we must consider how past errors deprived Burke and Wills of the opportunity of actually seeing the sea of the Gulf of Carpentaria. With current technology, we can now identify the major omission that was introduced by Stokes' assistant navigator Fitzmaurice and the major navigation time error by Leichhardt in the vicinity of the Flinders River.

Thevenot, on his maritime chart of the Gulf printed in 1663, showed the rivers entering the eastern shore of the Gulf. These were all, with one exception, identified by Flinders and Leichhardt. Leichhardt carried a copy of Arrowsmith's map of the continent of New Holland.[xvii] Leichhardt, who approached by land, particularly deserves credit for his identification as he did it under the most difficult circumstances, even though there is doubt about the present names used when compared with the Dutch.

The river that Stokes, Leichhardt and Arrowsmith failed to identify, or identify correctly as far as Leichhardt was concerned, was the Caron named by the Dutch, now called the Norman. Flinders identified it even though he was a long way offshore. His latitude and longitude location of the river mouth is only three miles out when compared with current maps.[xviii]

Gaps in Stokes' Work

Stokes carried out the close inshore work and delegated this section to Fitzmaurice. Stokes surveyed the Flinders and Albert Rivers in detail because the major reason for their research was to find maximum river access to the interior. Fitzmaurice, who was Assistant Surveyor/ship,[xix] surveyed the first two or three miles of the Bynoe then abandoned it with this note in Stokes' report: -

> large inlet...this was only examined a short distance in a south direction; but from the bank being thrown out six miles from its

mouth, with a channel nearly half way through, it evidently disembougues [sic] a large volume of water, aud [sic] we may reasonably infer it to be a river. xx

The Bynoe, at the point Fitzmaurice turned back, is a large river and roughly two hundred yards wide. Below is a photo of the Bynoe River taken at dawn.

Bynoe River

They named the feature Bynoe's Inlet after the ship's doctor. Note that Fitzmaurice did not definitely identify it as either a creek or a river. Seven miles east was another inlet, with a sandy beach extending to the southwest of it.xxi This inlet was the Caron of the Dutch, the Norman of today — also a large river.

Fitzmaurice was not as thorough or as zealous as his captain, even though he had several days to spare, and missed the opportunity to explore it. This in turn had a major effect on the accuracy of Leichhardt's plan and Burke and Wills' information. Stokes' written instructions from the Admiralty included: -

> As this question, whether there are or are not any rivers of magnitude on the western coast is one of the principal objects of the expedition, you will leave no likely opening unexplored, nor desist from its examination till fully satisfied;... to devote that part

> of the season to a more careful investigation of the low shores of the Gulf of Carpentaria, where it has been surmised, though very loosely, that rivers of some capacity will be found. [xxii]

This was added to in Volume 2: -

> and through, from your transient stay at any one place, you will often experience the mortification of leaving them incomplete, yet that should not discourage you in the collection of every useful fact within your reach. Your example in this respect will stimulate the efforts of the younger officers under your command, and through them may even have a beneficial influence on the future character of the navy. [xxiii]

Stokes was an enthusiast; he followed the Admiralty's instructions exactly and explored the Flinders and the Albert rivers with his usual meticulous attention to detail. His enthusiasm and poetic streak are reflected in his written word as he set out from his ship for the Albert River: -

> The ripples rolled rapidly, expanding from the boat's bows over the water, whilst the men stretched out as if unconscious of the exertion of pulling, every one of them feeling his share of the excitement. From the western sky the last lingering rays of the sun shot athwart the wave, turning it, as it were, by the alchemy of light into a flood of gold. Overhead the cope of the heaven was gradually growing soberer in hue from the withdrawal of those influences which lately had warmed and brightened it; but in the west a brilliant halo encircled the declining ruler of the day. [xxiv]

It should be noted that, in Stokes' time, officers were not involved in the rowing.

Fitzmaurice did not have this fire. Being less enthusiastic, and probably closer to the crew, he only explored the first two or three miles of the Bynoe, a larger river than the Flinders, although it is a tributary of the Flinders. The irony is that the river he missed to the east was the Caron/Yappar/Norman, the largest river flowing into the Gulf. Current navigators refer to this river as the Norman, but the Dutch first named it the Caron. Leichhardt found it but did not identify it as such; he had already found a small stream that he assumed to be the Caron as its direction matched Flinders notes. We now know this small stream as the Walker, which flows into the Norman nearly halfway upstream towards Normanton. Leichhardt named the Caron of the Dutch as the Yappar, a word the local Aboriginal People used.

This threatened Leichhardt's plan with a major error because the draftsman interpreted Stokes' failure to proceed up the Bynoe as the end of the river. Obviously, he did not read the report fully or did not appreciate its significance. Stokes' chart carries a note referring to the lack of time and that it could be a river. This was strangely ignored by the draftsman. The chart shows extensive mud flats out from the river's mouth, which is a common feature of the rivers in that area. Leichhardt, armed with this information, would have assumed that there was no river of significance between the Norman and the Flinders.

Fitzmaurice's subsequent journey up the coast cut through the Caron's (Norman's) more extensive mud flats. Stokes' chart shows that Fitzmaurice's route was a direct line to the Fitzmaurice River, the rendezvous point. He did not spend much time exploring. Arrowsmith also misidentified the Caron/Yappar as the Flinders and then showed Leichhardt's route as running down the eastern side of the Flinders when he was, in fact, west of it. This is in line with Leichhardt's false sighting of the sea.

Fitzmaurice, if he had followed his instructions, would have navigated up the Bynoe River to reach a similar latitude as his captain had navigated to in the Flinders River seven miles to the west. He would then have navigated up the Norman and recorded an accurate plan of the area that Leichhardt's journey would have fitted into He chose not to, instead heading straight to the rendezvous point where: -

> he had been seriously wounded in the ankle by the discharge of a gun which had gone off within a few yards of it. The accident having happened several days ago, and the whole charge of shot being buried in his foot, his sufferings were intense. It was thought for some time that amputation would be necessary; but though this was not the case, he was maimed for life.

> Mr. Fitzmaurice had fortunately, before he was disabled, completed his examination of the coast between the Flinders and Van Diemen's Inlet, with his usual praiseworthy activity. On leaving the former he found that the shore trended N.47°E., with a large inlet at the end of ten miles. This was only examined a short distance in a south direction; but from the bank being thrown out six miles from its mouth, with a channel nearly half way through, it evidently disembougues [sic] a large volume of water, aud [sic] we may reasonably infer it to be a river. It is named in the chart Bynoe's Inlet. Seven miles beyond was another inlet, with a sandy beach extending for two miles to the south-west of it. Five miles further, the trend of

the coast changed to N.4°E., continuing almost strait [sic] to Van Diemens Inlet, distant twenty-five miles; and, with the exception of the first five, is sandy throughout. xxv

The area where Fitzmaurice experienced his misfortune is now a well-known fishing spot named Accident Inlet to commemorate the incident. In retrospect, he probably wished he had spent his time exploring the area, as his instructions stated. He would almost certainly have saved himself from a serious injury.

Accident Inlet, before we were side-tracked by the story of Burke and Wills, was a favourite fishing spot for us. We caught many beautiful grunters, some thirty miles east from the port of Karumba located on the Norman River. On one notable occasion, we missed the inlet and motored a total of 66 nautical miles in an 11-foot tinny. Not the most comfortable of journeys, especially for the long-suffering wife who had the job of sitting at the bow of the vessel, which bounced up and down unmercifully. This experience resulted in the captain, David, driving nearly a thousand kilometres to Cairns to order a bigger tinny, a 16-foot plate aluminium boat, which did sterling service even after we switched from fishing to looking for traces of Burke and Wills, and later, Leichhardt.

No doubt, this purchase was mostly to mollify the long-suffering wife, although any excuse would do.

The new boat

After we got the new boat, we again fished at Accident Inlet where we were buzzed by a coast watch surveillance plane. As honest citizens, we obligingly sat on one side of our boat so that they could check our registration number on the other side.

John Lort Stokes rose through the ranks from his original midshipman's position as a twelve-year old to become an Admiral in the Royal Navy, becoming the first person to ever achieve that distinction from such a lowly beginning.[xxvi] He must have been disappointed that later explorations in the Gulf showed his work to be wanting in the area he delegated to Fitzmaurice and that, as a result, his chart was flawed, and major locations missed.

Leichhardt's Errors

These errors coupled with Leichhardt's longitude errors of 22' or 23' were included in the plan drawn by Arrowsmith. Leichhardt's error was most likely a watch error as the reliability of his watch was doubtful. In his recent book *Beyond Leichhardt*, Glen McLaren points out that the errors were much less at the Albert River. It was certainly accurate enough to get Leichhardt to his objective, Port Essington, which had to be the ultimate test for any navigator of that era.

As the mission was a success, no one could dispute the map at the time. Although Gregory pointed out an error of similar magnitude further west, which Wills may have known about. As Leichhardt had taken a complex route west of the Caron/Yappar/Norman, Wills could have speculated that any error of Leichhardt's would have been further west. He did not know of his 22' or 23' longitude error that we can now see on the AUSLIG maps. Wills' plot placed him further east, and this lines up with the stub of the Bynoe River as shown on Stokes' chart and Leichhardt's plan. Where Leichhardt's plan marks the Flinders River, he was actually on the Norman well to the east of Camp 119. His 22nd of July point is on the Bynoe and his 24th of July point is on the Flinders.

When Arrowsmith drew the map for Leichhardt, he used Leichhardt's information to upgrade Stokes' maritime chart by modifying the latitude and longitude with a little "adjustment". This is a reasonable practice if all the information is of equal reliability but certainly a disaster in the area shown as the "Flinders River". Leichhardt's plot of where he approached the "Flinders River" is completely wrong, and this information was crucial to Wills' navigation.

We can see the extent of this in detail on the composite map showing explorers' routes on the next page. If Fitzmaurice had completed the exploration of the two rivers, Leichhardt's discrepancy would have been controlled and Stokes' and Leichhardt's maps would have closely matched our more accurate, present day ones. Wills could draw no other conclusion with his resources than that he was on the east bank of the Flinders, as shown on the Leichhardt map.

If Leichhardt's actual route is compared with the Leichhardt/Arrowsmith map, you will see the major east–west shift. Walker searched the area less than one year later and also concluded that he was on the Flinders River (when he was on the Bynoe). He had arranged to meet Captain Norman (without success) who was on the Flinders but failed to realise the error. His latitude observation on Sunday 5th of January 1862 shows he thought that he was only a mile south of the meeting point[xxvii]. He blazed trees along the Bynoe (thinking it was the Flinders) and buried bottles containing notes for Captain Norman, all to no avail.

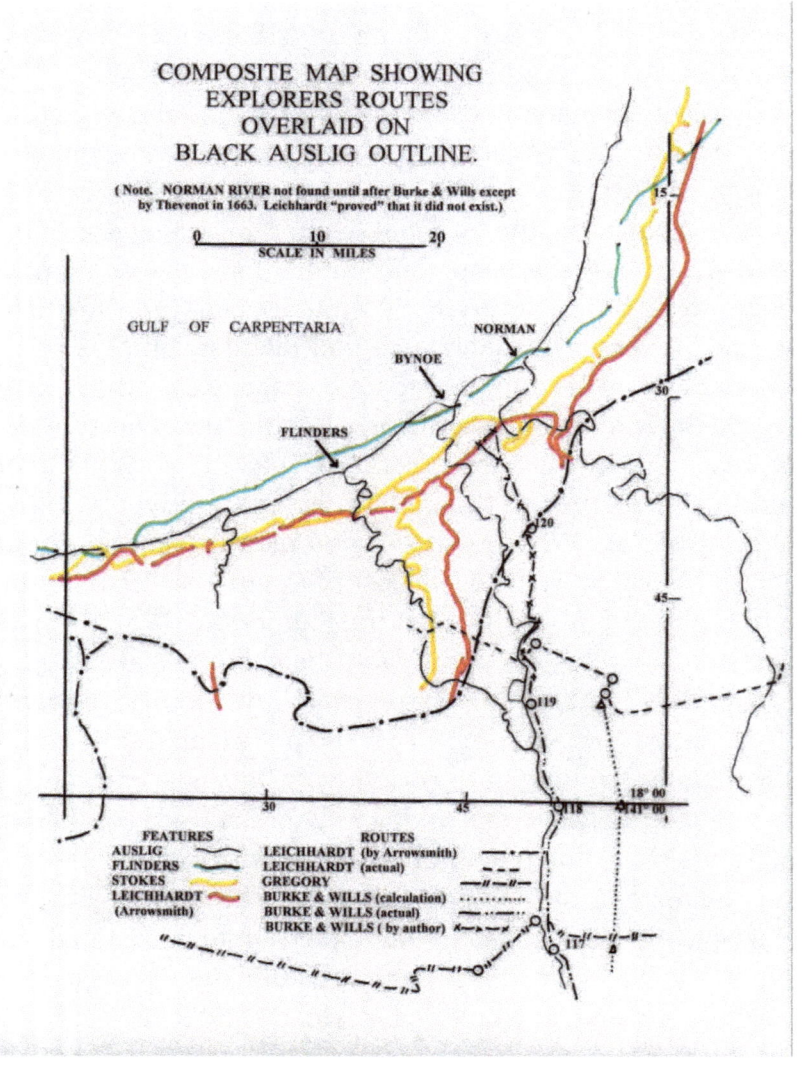

CHAPTER 8: PREVIOUS EXPLORERS

Imagine you had Wills' task of navigating to the shores of the Gulf in those times. According to Leichhardt's map, the only routes you would attempt would be along the Albert River or down the east bank of the Flinders River. From Stokes' chart, we see the latter option is the easiest. Both rivers sit on the same latitude according to Leichhardt's map so the distance would be identical either way. The map also showed that both rivers had been explored previously. In addition, according to the plan, Leichhardt had sighted the sea just north of the point reached at Camp 119 and had walked south to near the area of Camp 119. Wills had no way of knowing that all of these records were, in reality, for a different longitude.

I believe the existence of Leichhardt's map is the reason that Wills raised no concern about their drift fifty miles east. No doubt it was a considered decision and was confirmed by his daily observations. McKinlay, who led the South Australian Burke Relief Expedition, had a copy of Gregory's map [xxviii] and also a copy of Leichhardt's; how else would he assume that he had crossed Morning Inlet?[xxix] He had actually crossed the Saxby River near its junction with the Flinders. This also represents an error originating from Leichhardt's map.

Saxby — that reminds me of the day we travelled along several cattle station tracks to get to the Saxby Rodeo. Whenever you go through gates on a cattle station, or indeed on any farm, the rule is that you leave the gates as you found them, i.e., open or shut. On this occasion there were several closed gates, which the long-suffering wife was delegated to open and close.

This was not an arduous task. In fact, it gave me the chance to stretch my legs. But I did have a few choice bad words for one particular gate. The gate was easy to open but I had to hang onto it because it was inclined to swing back towards its closed position. Ah, I think, that will make it easier to close — I will just let it go.

I had not bargained on the trailing bit of wire that hooked under the cuff of my jeans and upended me on the dusty track into a most undignified position. I looked around hastily to see if anyone had witnessed my ungraceful performance and, of course, no-one was in sight. Even David, in the driver's seat, had not been looking in the rear-view mirror. I rolled around in the dust laughing for a while before dusting myself off and getting back into the truck as if nothing had happened.

At least I got a few good photos at the Rodeo

When John McKinlay crossed the Flinders River to search for Burke and Wills, he was about a mile away from Camp 116, and many miles south of the position represented by Logan Jack on his map. McKinlay missed their tracks near the Flinders River even though he explored a few miles upstream and downstream as indicated by his accurate plot of the river. We know he explored the area due to the continuous line on his plan, a contrast to his dotted line for estimations — which is a fairly standard survey practice.[xxx]

Arrowsmith also shows the mouth of the Flinders at 18.67 miles north of Camp 119. Wills would have deduced from this map that the total distance for the return journey north from Camp 120 was 37.25 miles plus deviations, i.e., in the low forties (latitude) and therefore attainable.

As the most recent map available, Leichhardt's plot influenced the German map mentioned previously. The German map is headed "provisional".[xxxi] It shows Burke and Wills' most northerly point near the Bynoe "stub", as identified by Fitzmaurice. It also shows Burke and Wills' route north in parallel with Leichhardt's journey south past the sea sighting. A perfectly normal assumption on the draftsman's part, which led to Burke and Wills' decision to try to reach the sea from Camp 119, taking just the horse and a few provisions with them.

The evidence in this chapter explains the actions of Burke and Wills over the next three days and the timing of their dash towards the Gulf.

CHAPTER 9
CAMP 119

Where did Burke and Wills camp for the nights of the 10th and 11th of February 1861? These two nights would have been at Camp 120. The two maps mentioned did not show a location for that camp. The Bush Tucker Man[i] relates that he had heard from an old stockman about a Burke and Wills blazed tree in the area forty years before; however, no one has found that tree since. I have heard the same story second-hand from locals but have not been able to determine the stockman's name.

The Stokes Range about two miles south of Camp 120

Tracking the Trees

A statement attributed to King claims "they took no knives or implements to do so"[ii] — meaning that there could be no marked trees north of Camp 119. I note the claim with minor reservations as other statements attributed to King at the same time raise some doubts. He stated that they blazed fifteen trees and cut a **B** on each of the trees at Camp 119.

Frederick Walker found only one tree with a **B** over **CXIX**,* one with **SE. E 14** and the remainder were only blazed. The blazed trees remaining in 1997 did not have a **B**. With one important exception, none remained by 1998; evidence suggests this is due to the use of chain saws and camping fires in the 1997–98 years. I only hope the people responsible enjoyed their campfires. The one exception is the original coolibah **B** over **CXIX** by Burke and Wills, which stands a short distance from the tree that Walker blazed, the two monuments and the cast lamp post. Initially, I had been told that the original **B** tree of Burke and Wills had long since disappeared, but I learned later in my research that it had been found by J.P. Thomson at the end of 1909/early 1910. Thomson took the precaution to record its position in relation to Walker's tree by compass bearing and measured distance. His visit to the area was sparked when the staff of Magowra station found Walker's marks from 1862 at the Burke and Wills' campsite together with the Burke and Wills' blazed tree.

Thomson, upon finding Camp 119 in 1909, described the **B** tree: -

> The exception proved to be a Coolibah, bearing by compass 274° 30', and distant one chain eighty-five and a half links from Walker's tree. A critical examination of the old mark on the Eastern side of this Coolibah, revealed the rather faint but clearly traceable outlines of the block letter B. Unlike the original marks on all the other trees, the shield cut out of the coolibah was only slightly overgrown, so that most of its surface had been left fully exposed to the wind and weather of a severe tropical climate for fully 48 years... Walker found a tree at what he at first fancied to be the same place marked B CXIX, being the more likely inscription for the explorers to have left behind them, at what was practically the objective point of their overland journey. Should this view be correct, and it is entirely borne out by the history of Australian exploration, then we are justified in assuming that the latter part of the inscription (CXIX), probably not so deeply cut as the former, must have naturally disappeared from the Coolibah tree. [iii]

---

* Burke and Wills only used Roman Numerals for camp numbers.

The "B" tree at Camp 119 in 1909 and 1999

This tree was re-identified in 1997 by Queensland surveyor Richard Cork using the notes and photo taken by Thomson. The tree has now grown over the mark. Given the state of the tree in 1909 and the time taken to grow over, this blaze should never be opened up as no useful purpose would be served. Indeed, the opposite would be the case as the tree's life would probably be shortened. As it is, we know that it is a certain link with Burke and Wills.

Walker, in his search for Burke and Wills the following December 1861 and again in January 1862, marked at least four trees and probably several others in the area between Camps 119 and 120. Later explorers have never found any of these trees except for the one on the site of Camp 119. To my knowledge, the only one found prior to my research is that tree blazed by Walker.

Walker's blazed tree at Camp 119

Rediscovered Blaze

I have since found a blazed tree identical in style and dimensions to Walker's tree at his campsite of the 8th–12th January 1862. (A photo of this is on the next page.) Walker describes his tree as 0.75 of a mile away from Burke and Wills' Camp 119. I recorded its GPS distance in a straight line as 0.46 of a mile and the walking distance as about 0.6 of a mile. It is also a coolibah tree, the same as the other two marked trees at Camp 119. Its growth patterns are similar. As a result of about three feet of erosion in the black soil creek, the tree had fallen over to the west, with most of the flexible roots intact, and the blaze now facing upwards.

Walker's camp within about half a kilometre of Camp 119

The plaque attached by David Hillan in 1998

This change would have occurred not long after the tree had been marked, judging by the limited timber growth. Another limb of the tree had taken over the tree's growth and the tree was alive and healthy when we found it. Where the tree once faced to the east is probably the exact location of the campsite on the east bank of the creek.

My search for Walker's missing blazed tree started at the downstream end of the water hole in what could be called Billy's Creek East. Working my way upstream, I inspected a myriad of trees. I decided that this method could be a waste of time and started to think more logically.

In the end, I located the tree using the following logic: Walker's camp would have been near the upstream end of the water hole where the fresh water ran in, as the horses in the camp would have stirred up the water with the black mud. After I walked some distance up along the banks, I decided that this was the point where I would have camped, because it was upstream and hence ensured clean water. I turned around to find that the blaze was in full view merely six yards away. I was stunned. Its position is latitude 17° 52' 26", longitude 140° 49' 42".* Walker did not record a numbered tree at this campsite, but he marked one at Camp 119 instead. The fact that Camp 119 had been discovered only at the end of Walker's stay could explain the lack of record and numbering in Walker's diary. The exposed face of the tree's blaze has only weathered by about one inch.

Is this the tree that the mysterious stockman claimed to have seen? Perhaps. Ludwig Leichhardt may also have marked a tree at his campsite just to the east of the Bynoe or at his crossing of the Bynoe just north of 119. The stockman could have seen one of these. Such a tree was found on the 17th of September 1864 by Macdonald to the west at his camp number 17: -

> Near our camp I observed a box tree marked L, which I suppose to be one of poor Leichhardt's. It has evidently been cut a number of years, and the mark is nearly grown out.[iv]

He also marked a tree at that campsite. His mark was an **M** with a carved ⌒, or eyebrow, over the top it and with the camp number below the **M**.

Macdonald's maps conflict with current ones regarding his latitudes. His map refers to saltwater — non-existent at the latitude he recorded — and the width of the river at that point conflicts with present information. I believe that Macdonald was further north than shown on his map.

---

*All my GPS positions are on the WGS 84 datum for long term practical compatibility with the Australian datum after the year 2000

CHAPTER 10
WILLS' NAVIGATION SKILLS

I assembled information from as many sources as possible to better understand Burke and Wills' journey north from Camp 119. This campsite is a well-known location on the local tourist circuit with its blazed tree and monument. Thus, it is a known starting point.

Burke and Wills travelled north from Camp 119 on the 10th of February 1861. Their horse Billy was "lightly loaded" for a dash to the Gulf and they left the other party members behind. King, the sole survivor of the Expedition did not accompany them. Therefore, the only available information is contained in Wills' field notes, corroborated by King with his second-hand knowledge at the subsequent Commission of Inquiry in Melbourne. The notes for the 10th of February are detailed; however, the only comment in Wills' field notes covering the 11th of February was: -

> Next morning we started at daybreak, leaving the horse short hobbled.[i]

Whilst Wills' description of the 10th of February[ii] is possibly the most detailed daily record by Wills for the whole journey, I found that it was hard to relate to the area according to current maps. Prior to the issue of more recent maps, getting an accurate overview was next to impossible. All researchers seem to have had the same difficulty. Many researchers have suggested that Wills overestimated the distance they travelled and that Saltwater Creek, which they had to cross on the way, would have been impassable due to the Wet and king tides. I have been told that Saltwater Creek cannot be crossed anywhere in this area.

However, after examining all the information and being on site, I deemed these observations as incorrect. In fact, Wills' estimation of distance was highly accurate as was his description of the land. I did not reach these conclusions quickly or lightly. First, I needed to consider the following questions.

Are Wills' written words along with Frederick Walker's from his subsequent investigation several months later the only clues we have, or can we deduce more?

Who was Wills? What was his experience? How reliable was his work? Was he prone to exaggeration? Can modern technology assist in further understanding? Can the researcher enter his mind?

Reliability of Estimated Distances

Surveyors work with repetitive measurements and soon develop skills at estimating distances accurately. Wills, in his previous employment and during the Expedition, had considerable experience in this area. When travelling longer distances, surveyors sometimes track the time that they are on the move. Captain John Lort Stokes describes this practice in his exploration of the Victoria River.

> We estimated our distance from the boats, having carefully timed ourselves each march, at 23 miles. [iii]

John McKinlay also used this method with great skill for his Burke Relief Expedition (despite the shortcomings of his watch).

> Monday, May 26 - Camp 5. I find that my watch - the only one in going order, or rather disorder, gains eleven minutes in the hour with the regulator hard back to slow - now and then -, without any apparent cause it stops; until by sundry shakings and bumps it is prevailed upon to go again - which is most unsatisfactory, situated as I am here in calculating distances… Started at 8:15am, on bearing of 95.5°; at 9:17 passed till this time thickly wooded (low), small ironstone, pebbly country, well grassed-ridges on both sides; at 9:17 entered open plains;…at 11:14, lagoon apparently about one mile south. [iv]

Some surveyors count the steps they take, averaged at one yard. This is a common practice of surveyors when looking for old survey marks. William Landsborough used this system in his search for Burke and Wills. In one instance he quoted on a seven-mile leg.

> By counting my steps I made the distance seven miles to a bend of the Albert River near which Mr Moore's ponds are situated, and two miles and three quarters further brought us to the point near which the ship had reached. [v]

Robert Logan Jack was a professional geologist charged with producing fairly accurate geological maps. Even he was acutely aware of the hurdles to producing a realistic map. In a professional assessment of the problem, he states: -

> The first lesson to force itself upon me was that my estimates of distances covered had been influenced by fatigue or difficulties on the one hand (leading to over-estimation) or by good-going and

good-feeding for the horses on the other (leading to under-estimation).

The second lesson was that, even in the direction of my course, I had in many instances strayed to the right or left, as a ship may steer a definite course and yet make leeway owing to the pressure of forces incorrectly estimated, or even not recognised. In short, the personal equation had to be introduced and allowed for before I could hope to reconcile my supposed with my actual position on any given date. [vi]

Current-day geologists and surveyors have the luxury of working with accurate survey or GPS control.

Surveyors are never lost — just temporarily geographically displaced

Technology has progressed even further. At the time of this book's publication, many new cars and most phones have inbuilt GPS. I often use my phone's GPS to find my way around the city where I now live. The GPS voice has been christened Myrtle and she is not infallible. She has driven me around in circles more than once and sometimes even instructed me to do a U-turn on a busy freeway. On our last trip north, after David could no longer drive due to failing eyesight, she happily ordered me into a big building site. The workmen did not notice for a while because I was driving a white Toyota much like all the other work vehicles on the site. Finally, they noticed our off-road van attached and waved us back. My driving skills were severely tested as I reversed our rig up an incline and around a bend.

A surveyor's distance estimates are normally checked against latitude and longitude, or other control measurements, and are not used as survey data. For a surveyor, this process would only be a personal competition with himself for interest and as an aid in making some decisions. The main problem with the step-counting method is, if used too much, it can make it difficult to get to sleep at night — counting sheep will not help. Your companions wonder why you will not talk to them; replies to their questions are delayed while you mentally save the information, otherwise your tedious work will be lost.

A surveyor has absolutely no reason to exaggerate. Wills checked his estimates with latitude and longitude observations and, as he was proceeding mainly north, he didn't need to make any complicated longitude checks and could trust the accuracy of the latitudes over longer distances.

Checking Distances

The only distance of Wills that I have been able to check is the distance between Camps 84 to 86. To quote Wills' notes: -

> Saturday, 5th January, 1861.- On leaving Camp 84 ...At a distance of about two miles in a N.N.E. direction, we came to a shallow waterhole... The camels and horses being greatly in need of a rest, we moved up about half a mile, and camped for the day...Sunday, 6th January, 1861. As we proceeded up in a northerly direction, we found the waterhole to diminish in size very much, and at about two and a half miles the creek ran out... As there was no sign of timber to the north, we struck off to N.W. by N. for a fine line that came up from the S.W... At a distance of about three miles, we reached the bank of a fine creek containing a sheet of water two chains broad.[vii]

Wills' descriptions of the three routes of 2.5 miles N.NE, then 3.0 miles N, then 3.0 miles NW by N computes to a latitude change of 7.03'. But when Wills observed latitudes at Camps 84 and 86, the latitude change was only 3'. Wills made no attempt to adjust these figures to make them agree. He was confident that his distance estimations were better than his observations and he recorded no comment on the difference.

Using the distance between the two water holes and the latitude and longitude, we can speculate that the waterholes Wills was at were, according to the AUSLIG map on the SPRINGVALE sheet, Cockatoo and Old Station. To be certain about Wills' estimation I had to make a ground visit and identify the campsites by their marked trees and measure the distances for myself. I found that his estimations were indeed superior to his survey observations.

The only other distance available for comment is between Camp 119 and Billy's Creek. Wills uses the words "a few hundred yards".[viii] The GPS shows this to be about 1090 yards in a direct line, but a walking route would be at least 1200 yards. Certainly, Wills did not exaggerate this distance — in fact, he probably under-estimated. The GPS distance is much longer than my understanding of a few hundred yards; I thought it would be in the order of under a half mile. The accurate GPS distance does explain why they did not involve the two Expedition members at the base camp to help them extricate the horse Billy when he got bogged crossing the creek that now bears his name.

This was a point that had puzzled me. Although Billy's Creek was not otherwise an area of significance, it does give an insight into Wills' distance estimates: Wills was not prone to exaggeration.

Some early explorers used pedometers, both for people and camels. An example of each of these is held in the Survey Museum, Adelaide. This type of instrument reduced a significant amount of the guesswork about position information, yet not enough to reach acceptable survey standards. We do not know if pedometers were available in 1860; however, their existence highlights early explorers' and travellers' efforts to find a mechanical solution to estimate distances.

CHAPTER 11
NAVIGATION INSTRUMENTS

We have a wealth of information on Burke and Wills, including Wills' navigation notes and comments from others as detailed later. The originals of *A Successful Exploration through the Interior of Australia from Melbourne to the Gulf of Carpentaria from the Journals of William John Wills* edited by his father, William Wills, still exist in family records. The book contains reports from the journey as well as excerpts from the Royal Commission. The book establishes Wills' interest in surveying and how he became involved in it through his interest in and aptitude for mathematics.

Wills' father offered to give him a set of surveying equipment, and the specifications he supplied to his father[i] showed that Wills either possessed good knowledge or had taken good advice. He knew the field problems of lightheaded and thus unstable tripods and his remedy showed practical field experience. The fact that he requested from his father a "Troughton's best reflecting circle, eight-inch radius, divided on silver" confirms the written record of his interest in astronomy. This type of instrument lost favour to the sextant, probably due to bulk and fragility as it is a full circle sixteen inches in diameter and includes fragile fittings.

I have never seen one of these in a collection and reference to one is hard to find. One is kept in The Harvard University Collection of Historical Scientific Instruments photo on page 370 of *The Quest for Longitude*, edited by William J.H. Andrews. Another is shown on page 44 of *Nautical Antiques & Collectables* by Jon Baddeley. The circle would probably be suited as a base camp instrument, but not one to be carried and used frequently. An equivalent sextant of the same radius is only one sixth the size and weight of the circle. However, the circle would have had an accuracy advantage since different sections of the circle could reduce the error caused by the engraving on the measuring scale.

If you look at the engraving on an object, you will notice that it is grooved. The question is, which exact point in the groove do you measure from? When I undertook a navigation course at the South Australian Sea Rescue Squadron, it surprised me how fine the measurements had to be to ensure accuracy. We used charts for plotting a boat's course (this was before the days of GPS) and our pencils had to be very sharp because the width of the pencil line drawn on the chart could cause our reckonings to be out by quite a margin. Such an error was not acceptable if we were looking for a person in the water or even a small boat in rough seas.

I undertook the course after David stopped the boat when we were out fishing in Gulf St Vincent and announced that he had a heart attack and could I please take him back to the ramp. I looked around, could not see the shore, the skies were cloudy and I did not know how to read a chart. I told him not to be silly and when we returned to shore, I signed up for the Sea Rescue navigation course immediately.

The observing technique used in that era is still used today, just with current surveying instruments. However, Wills was probably able to eliminate the same error on sextants by calibration observations, which he certainly carried. He left a copy at the Observatory in Melbourne for his Lohmin of Hamburg divided 10"[ii] sextant. The fact that he specified Lohmin indicates that he might have had a second sextant. If that were the case, then the second sextant was most likely abandoned at Camp 32 Return.

> Wednesday, 20th March 1861. Camp 32R...The packs we overhauled and left nearly 60 lb. weight of things behind. They were all suspended from a shrub close to the creek. [iii]

There is a remarkable parallel between this field note entry and the story told by explorer Andrew Hume, who was mentioned previously in connection with the Roper Bar river crossing. Hume claimed to have found papers in the northern area: -

> rolled in a piece of blanket then a piece of oil cloth, and this was covered with tea-tree bark, and the whole lot put into a saddle bag, and that bag put into another bag. The quadrant and thermometer is lying above them on the shelf of rock, in a little bit of a box,[iv] together with other things such as pistols and a small axe.

Few explorers would abandon a navigation instrument without a spare or in the circumstance outlined by Hume. Could there be a connection? Hume crossed Burke and Wills' route in this general area. The papers that Hume described were wrapped in tea-tree bark, large sheets of which existed further north near the Flinders River on Burke and Wills' route.

Another possibility is that these survey instruments belonged to Ludwig Leichhardt's final expedition, but I find that unlikely. As Leichhardt carried a sextant on his successful northern expedition from near Brisbane to Port Essington in 1845, it would be strange if he had reverted to the use of a quadrant on his final expedition. Hume may not have known the difference between some instruments, and so I have discounted his theory.

Wills carried a group of similar navigation instruments. In order of bulk, weight and probably accuracy was the circle, then the sextant and then the octant. The octant was often called the quadrant due to the scale engraving. This can cause confusion with a much earlier and simpler instrument that was the true quadrant. The sextant proved to be the most popular due to its observing range and it is still in use as I write, while the others are now curiosities. The octant could not observe higher stars with a reflection from an artificial horizon, which was required for land navigation. A person with no navigating experience would not easily identify an instrument as a quadrant, octant or sextant, therefore Hume possibly found a sextant rather than a quadrant or octant. However, these abandoned instruments are open to further research.

Wills' Additional Credentials

Wills worked on country surveys[v] firstly in the office under District Surveyor Taylor, then with Surveyor Byerley of the Survey Department under the same District Surveyor. This employment occurred while under the supervision of the Victorian Surveyor General.[vi] Wills' letters to his family contained these names; we can confirm these names with a recently published book that details the early years of surveying in Victoria.[vii] Wills then obtained a position as Assistant to Professor Neumayer at the Magnetic Observatory — as distinct from the Astronomical Observatory — at Melbourne[viii] where he eventually lived in.[ix] This position was offered to Wills on the recommendation of the Surveyor General.[x] Letters to his family showed that he was very interested in scientific matters.[xi]

Wills had greater experience in astronomy than most surveyors his age, more even than many surveyors experience in a lifetime. He was clearly held in high esteem by the Surveyor General and the Director of the Observatory, both having provided very significant recommendations.

While Wills had a great deal of experience in the field, we have seen inexperienced tourists, following their retirement dream of a trip around Australia in a big brand-new caravan, do some crazy things on outback roads. Huge road trains frequent these roads — sometimes over fifty metres long and weighing nearly two hundred tonnes. They can have two or three trailers attached and are often shod with up to eighty tyres. They travel at speed and you can imagine how long it takes for such a big rig to pull up.

Outback road courtesy demands that other road users head for the bush when they see one of these monsters coming towards them on a dirt track or single lane of bitumen. This is what we have always done. However, we have seen tourists (or grey nomads as they are fondly called in this country) stick like glue to the middle of the road, forcing a road train off onto the verge. In doing this, the tourist is risking a shattered windscreen, or worse, an overturned road train.

Wills was subsequently appointed to the Expedition as Surveyor and Astronomer[xii] and later as second in charge. Astronomer was a somewhat misleading title as the only stellar observation instrument that records show they took is a seven-inch sextant. As previously mentioned, he possibly carried a backup sextant (he also had backup thermometers, barometers, chronometers and artificial horizons).[xiii]

Finding a Level Horizon

The seven-inch sextant of that era was a basic navigation instrument. An eight-inch instrument was more accurate and appears to be the most common size in use at the time. A sextant is mainly a ship's navigation device used to measure angles. Essentially, it is a 60° protractor with a vernier scale to allow an accurate reading of angles. While reading the angle of elevation to a star, the sea horizon gives a level reference. Navigators then corrected results for refraction of light, height above water and for the earth's curvature if the horizon was visible. Inland use requires the aid of an artificial horizon, which is a small standalone mirror device that can be levelled with a special level or by the use of a small mercury pond measuring 4.5 by 2.5 inches. (See photo page 98.) Wills carried both on the Expedition.

The mercury pond must be set up in such a way that, from the sextant, both the star, (or sun or moon) and its reflection in the pond can be seen. The mean, i.e., the average of the number of observations taken, gives the vertical angle from level (without the usual corrections, such as for curvature of the earth) to the sea horizon. But a mercury artificial horizon is difficult to use. Dust on the surface of the mercury pond, even after a few minutes, can cause a problem of lost visibility. The mirror that goes with it must also be small enough to carry without breaking or flexing and must have the surface ground accurately. Because it is small, it is hard to bring the reflection into view. Another method that Wills tried was the reflection off a still lagoon: -

> Finding two or three waterholes of good milky water we camped for the night. This enabled me to secure an observation of the eclipse of Jupiter's satellite, as well as some latitude observations. The night was so calm that I used the water as an horizon; but I find it more satisfactory to take the mercury for several reasons. [xiv]

The sextant was likely handheld by Wills. The accuracy falls far short of what a current theodolite will do. It is also much harder to use in the dark of night. Wills' preference for mercury avoided the problem of levelling the artificial horizon and then reversing the device without disturbing the base, although he still had to reverse the triangular ground glass cover for half of the observations.

Mercury was tricky to transport. It had to be stored in an iron container within the artificial horizon box. Mercury expands a significant amount with minimal temperature increase, hence its use in thermometers. It must therefore be in a container less than full and kept out of direct sun.

Mercury can become dangerous if spilt. Moist air also provides a challenge when using mercury because a black scum forms, blocking reflection. This can be removed by wiping with cardboard or dissolved by a drop of potassium cyanide. In very wet weather the moisture in the air makes it difficult, and in many cases impossible, to use a mercury horizon. Wills took latitude and longitude observations on the journey down the Corella River. Therefore, we can be almost certain that it was not constantly raining.

Night observations of stars also presented a unique problem in the northern area, which Wills would have encountered.

John Lort Stokes records that: -

> I got the requisite observation for latitude during the night; and since necessity is ever the mother of invention, read off my sextant by torch made for the occasion from pieces of paper bark. It will easily be believed, that I did not needlessly prolong the work; for the light of the torch rendered me a prominent mark for any prowling savage to hurl his spear at. [xv]

Stokes was rather sensitive about being attacked as Lewis, Roper, Fitzmaurice and Charles Keys had narrowly escaped from being speared as they checked the compass for variation while ashore. Stokes describes the incident: -

> The observations had been commenced, and were about half completed, when on the summit of the cliffs, which rose about twenty feet above their heads, suddenly appeared a large party of natives with poised and quivering spears, as if about immediately to deliver them. Stamping on the ground, and shaking their heads to and fro, they threw out their long shaggy locks in a circle, whilst their glaring eyes flashed with fury as they champed and spit the ends of their long beards. They were evidently in earnest, and bent on mischief. It was, therefore, not a little surprising to behold this paroxysm of rage evaporate before the happy presence of mind displayed by Mr. Fitzmaurice, in immediately beginning to dance

and shout, though in momentary expectation of being pierced by a dozen spears. In this he was imitated by Mr. Keys who was assisting in the observations, and who at the moment was a little distance off, and might have escaped. Without, however, thinking of himself, he very nobly joined his companion in amusing the natives; and they succeeded in diverting them from their evident design. [xvi]

This incident was not sufficient warning for Stokes as he was caught out himself. He described it as follows: -

I had just turned my head round to look after my followers when I was suddenly staggered by a violent and piercing blow about my left shoulder: and ere the dart had ceased to quiver in its destined mark, a loud yell, such as the savage only can produce, told me by whom I had been speared. One glance sufficed to shew [sic] me the cliffs, so lately the abode of silence and solitude, swarming with the dusky forms of natives, now indulging in all the exuberant action which the Australian testifies his delight. One tall bushy-headed fellow led the group, and was evidently my successful assailant. I drew out the spear, which had entered the cavity of the chest, and retreated, with all the swiftness I could command, in the hope of reaching those who were coming up from the boat, and were then about half way... while at every respiration, the air escaping through the orifice of the wound... I spent the last struggling energy I possessed to join them. [xvii] *(See below.)*

Capt. Stokes speared, at Point Pearce

CHAPTER 11: NAVIGATION INSTRUMENTS

Equipment in the Field

Gregory and Leichhardt both used sextants while Flinders and Stokes both used a theodolite [xviii] for control observations from shore positions to supplement and control sea-borne sextant observations. Flinders had five sextants, one five-inch, one nine-inch and three eight-inch.[xix]

Stokes also had two sextants, one large and one small.[xx] Leichhardt had only one sextant of unknown radius.[xxi] In relation to Burke and Wills, a theodolite was mentioned by Manning Clark[xxii] and repeated by Michael Cathcart.[xxiii] However, in this instance I believe Clark wrote generally about explorers and exploration and was not referring specifically to Wills. Wills would not have required the mercury or other means to identify artificial horizons if he had a theodolite because it contains level bubbles.

David Hillan demonstrating the use of a theodolite

An old sextant like the one used by Wills

To better understand the difficulty of observation with a sextant and artificial horizon, let me quote from a textbook: -

> In the measurement of altitude, the artificial horizon is placed on the ground in front of the observer and at a convenient distance for the sighting of the reflected image. The latter is viewed directly. By moving the index arm the celestial body is then brought down until the two images are approximately in contact. This preliminary sighting should preferably be done with the blank tube, or simply through the telescope collar, and when the index arm is clamped at the approximate angle, the inverting telescope is screwed on as quickly as possible, and the two images are made coincident by the tangent screw. ... The use of a sextant stand is helpful, but if this is not available, the observer should sit on the ground and rest the right arm against the knee. [xxiv]

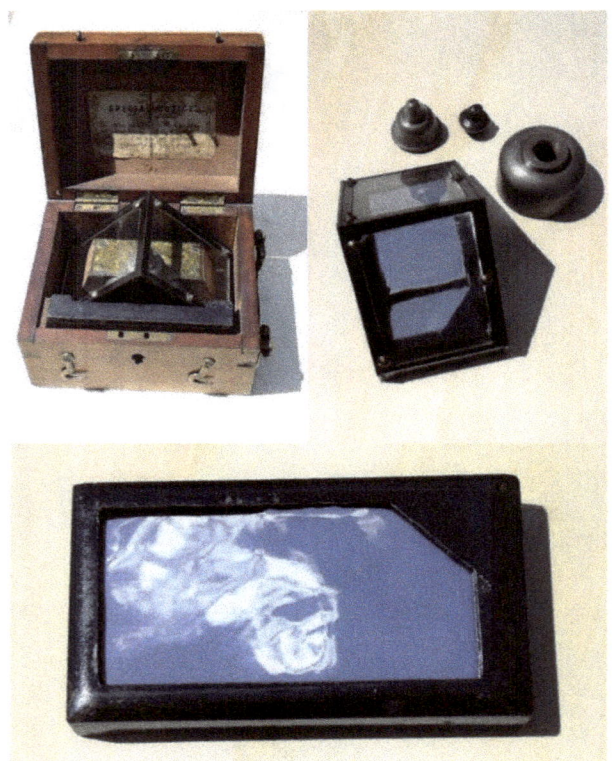

Artificial Horizon; the reflecting surface is mercury so absolute stillness is essential forgood readings

All of this is required for multiple observations, which includes reversing the glass cover on the artificial horizon for half the readings without moving the artificial horizon. This is no mean feat if it is on the ground or on a rock. Stokes also reported trouble in finding a suitable support for his artificial horizon: -

> I here again felt the inconvenience of our not being furnished with one of the pendulum horizons, invented by Captain Becher, R.N. It being high water, and as the shore was lined with an impenetrable growth of mangroves, we were unable to land. In vain did I try, by cutting down some of them, to find a rest for the artificial horizon on one of the stumps; they were so connected with each other beneath the water, by a perfect network of roots, that although several of the surrounding trees were felled, a tremulous motion was still conveyed from a distance, and I consequently lost the observation for latitude. [xxv]

It is not known if Wills had a sextant stand. Flinders used one for onshore observations in "most of the cases."[xxvi]

Wills travelled with limited resources. Even today, due to distance and sparse population, resources are limited, and replacements take a long time to arrive from the nearest big town, which can often be more than a thousand kilometres away.

We saw a utility truck on a station once with a shattered windscreen. The driver had punchedout a hole so that he could see to drive. Replacing a windscreen when you live on a remote outback station is not a simple or quick matter. He had considered his dog as well and had punched out a smaller hole in front of the passenger seat for it (although, perhaps the second hole was so that he didn't have his little mate leaning over to sharethe view).

Sometimes, when all else fails, Mitre 11 can help out. In Australia there is a chain of handymen stores called Mitre 10. In remote country areas, the local dump is nicknamed Mitre 11 and has been known to yield gold in the form of bits and pieces that can be used to repair important things such as axles.

Wills carried out his duties of navigating the party north and returning it to Coopers Creek base camp very professionally. Perhaps one of the reasons that Wills did not record many observations on the way back was because there was no need from a navigational point of view. Added to that, they would have been travelling as quickly as possible because they were late for a rendezvous with the relief party at Coopers Creek.

Some criticise Wills for not carrying out other general astronomy work. These critics likely did not know, or were not aware, of practical difficulties in the field: difficulties with the equipment that he carried, with the weather during the Wet season and with fatigue after long days and nights when they travelled by moonlight. Also, the whole objective of the Expedition changed at Coopers Creek when it became a dash for the Gulf. They could no longer fit observations that required a lot of time into their schedule. It was not only some equipment that had to be abandoned but most of the scheduled astronomical work as well.

A classic example of incorrect assumptions by inexperienced people is set out in the recently discovered, translated from German and published diary of Hermann Beckler, *A Journey to Coopers Creek*. Beckler was the Expedition's botanist. He left the Expedition after considerable dissatisfaction with Burke's directives about what had to be done by all members of the team. Later, he re-joined the relief party heading north to Coopers Creek. They lost the track and had to work hard together to survive, though sadly not all party members did survive. Beckler's actions and diary entries highlighted that he needed diverse skills to survive and that he did not have the time to devote solely to scientific studies. While he had once questioned Burke's decisions, Beckler eventually understood the realities of field work in remote and hostile environments.

Accuracy of Wills

Wills demonstrates his attention to detail in other ways, such as when he describes in his field notes an encounter with a bird that: -

> nearly resembles a cock pheasant in plumage, but in other respects it bears more the character of the magpie or crow, — all feathers and claws. [xxvii]

His description of what we now know as the Pheasant Coucal is accurate.[xxviii] A long-time local has confirmed to me that Wills' description of their eating qualities is also correct. The Pheasant Coucal is the least intelligent bird I have ever seen in the bush and a poor flier — I imagine it might now be extinct if it were a good source of food. Flinders seems to confirm Wills' view as he shows detailed knowledge of the eating qualities of the Bustard and turtle yet groups the "cookoo-pheasant [sic]" with cockatoos, gulls and crows.[xxix] The eating qualities of the latter three are enshrined into Australian folklore — each is to be boiled with a stone until the stone is soft at which point it is recommended to eat the stone.

CHAPTER 11: NAVIGATION INSTRUMENTS

Pheasant Coucal, photo by Erica Siegel

On another memorable occasion, I found some of this bird's feathers on the track and decided that I would like to have them in the band of my hat. Someone (not saying who) decided that it would be a good idea to superglue them together in a nice arrangement. I arranged them nicely and held them while David proceeded to superglue them together, in the process attaching my fingers as well. It was a long and mostly silent trip to the nearest town to purchase some solvent to unglue them.

My hat looked something like this

At another time, while travelling slowly along a rough bush track, one of these ungainly birds fluttered out of a tree and onto the track in front of us. Instead of flying up when it saw our vehicle, it ran awkwardly down the track in front of us, looking first over one shoulder, then the other. Eventually, it had the sense to take off and find cover in the bush. We had a good laugh when it almost overbalanced while landing on a tree branch.

Wills also describes an encounter with a large snake. Stories about snakes fall into the same category as stories about fish. The evidence is never produced for verification and is often exaggerated. To quote his words: -

> In crossing a creek by moonlight, Charley rode over a large snake; he did not touch him, and we thought it was a log until he struck it with the stirrup iron; we then saw that it was an immense snake, larger than any I have ever before seen in a wild state. It measured eight feet four inches in length and seven inches in girth around the belly; it was nearly the same thickness from the head to within twenty inches of the tail; it then tapered rapidly. The weight was 11½ pounds. From the tip of the nose to five inches back, the neck was black, both above and below; throughout the rest of the body, the under part was yellow, and the sides and back had irregular brown traverse bars on a yellowish brown ground. xxx

They ate it at the next camp (C16 Return), which they named Feasting Camp. Their food supplies were extremely low by then.

They did not know if the snake was poisonous although Wills doubted that it was, due to the teeth configuration: "I could detect no poisonous fangs"[xxxi]. Burke did not believe Wills as he was sick for a couple of days[xxxii] although no other party member became ill. This caused some delay on their return journey. That delay alone was more than sufficient to cost them their lives. Wills' description matches that of the: -

> Black Headed Python, it grows to three metres (10 feet), predominantly nocturnal. When provoked it raises the fore-body, flicks the tongue, hisses loudly and lunges as if to bite. [xxxiii]

I met one of these once on the side of the road and stopped to have a look. It did all the above and certainly confined me to the vehicle with windows up. It was one of only three or four aggressive snakes that I have ever encountered in the bush and I have seen hundreds — and that is not a fish story.

Incidentally, Wills was correct, it is not venomous.

This snake was described by Krefft in 1864 and he was credited with its discovery. One could argue that Wills should be given that honour.

The incident of the pheasant and of the snake documented by Wills in his field notes illustrate the accuracy of his descriptions without any embellishments.

This is a similar snake that we met while walking through the bush

CHAPTER 12
TO THE LAST CAMP

Between Camps 118 and 119, the Flinders River turned northwest so Burke and Wills followed another river, now known as the Bynoe, which was a branch of the Flinders River. Camp 119 was actually alongside the Little Bynoe, which takes a shortcut across a loop of the Bynoe River. The Flinders–Bynoe junction is well concealed and Frederick Walker missed it in his search for Burke and Wills.

When they made a dash from Camp 119 towards the sea, they took just three days' supply of food. This indicates that they were confident of reaching their goal in less than a day and a half. After all, they thought Ludwig Leichhardt, along with cattle, had already walked the same route without any problems. Leichhardt's report and his map would have shown them that. It also showed that they were less than nineteen miles from the sea. In reality, by the AUSLIG map, it is about twenty-seven miles, keeping to the east of the Bynoe, at the closest point.

Understanding the Area

With the aid of AUSLIG maps, we can plot Leichhardt's journey around the Normanton area to within a few miles and identify the major river he mentions as the Norman (Yappar or the Caron). We can also see where he crossed the Walker River (which he identified as the Caron), find his Norman River crossing area and find the creeks of Stockyard and Nineteen Mile where he had camped, as well as the creek just short of the Bynoe and then the Bynoe River itself, which he crossed on a bar about four miles north of Camp 119.

Leichhardt's descriptions of southerly travel were accurate due to latitude observations, but his westerly travel was substantially less reliable due to difficulties in determining longitude and his poor estimation of distance travelled. This poor distance estimation occurred on the westerly section from the Norman River to Stockyard Creek and beyond. Prior to this, while travelling mainly north–south sections, his longitude observations were his master and his recorded distances tied in with his latitudes.

Leichhardt's plotting shows that he had a longitude error of 22 or 23 minutes (about 21 miles). Wills did not have this knowledge. Therefore, any hopes entertained by the Expedition party of seeing the sea would have been a mirage.

The "sea" was reported by Leichhardt as follows: -

CHAPTER 12: TO THE LAST CAMP

> Charley rode through the dry mangrove scrub and came on a
> sandy beach with the broad ocean before him. [i]

Charley, his tracker from the Aboriginal Bathurst tribe, saw what he thought was the sea. In fact, he stood near what is now the Normanton–Karumba road at about the Eleven Mile Creek. This location is at an elevation of about eight metres and is twenty miles from the sea at Karumba. Apart from intervening trees, the curvature of the earth would have given a sighting distance to the horizon of about seven miles (for a six-foot tall person on a flat surface the distance is about three miles or five kilometres). The sea was well out of sight from this point; the report was a false sighting, indeed perhaps a mirage? Each day, Charley acted as a food forager and forward scout, in an area he did not know because he was not a local, on horseback while the others followed droving the cattle. Charley, after the sighting, backtracked and diverted the others south. He was the sole witness of what he thought was the sea.

Other information I found useful included tide details for the area at that time. Tides in Australia are computed at the National Tidal Facility, The Flinders University of South Australia in Adelaide. Tides are forecast in advance so looking into the past was a change. They computed the tides for me based on Karumba for February 1861.

To use this information, we simply needed to observe times at designated points along the coast and allow similar differences for the same points in 1861. Bi-monthly cycles of high tides coupled with high rains would slow down the runoff. The tide chart shows that, at the time in question, the tide cycle was dropping but was only two or three days from the peak. It also showed that the tide at Karumba was high around midnight and low around midday. The tidal range on those days was 2.2 to 3.0 metres, i.e., less than the range of a king tide. We will explore the significance of this later as we attempt to interpret Burke and Wills' movements. (See tide charts for the two days on page 131.)

What does all this information reveal about where Burke and Wills were on the nights of the 10th and the 11th of February 1861?

The area where they were is within Magowra Station, which is best referenced today on AUSLIG map MAGOWRA 7062 at a scale of 1:100 000, relevant part shown on next page. AUSLIG also supplied me with vertical air photos, namely Burketown, film number CAB 4015, prints 3065, 66, 67, 3079, 80, 3341, 42, 43 and 44. These were flown in June 1966 at 25 thousand feet. Stereoscopic pairs of air photos or an air photo mosaic greatly enhance the chances of interpreting Wills' field notes. They give moredetail than a two-dimensional map.

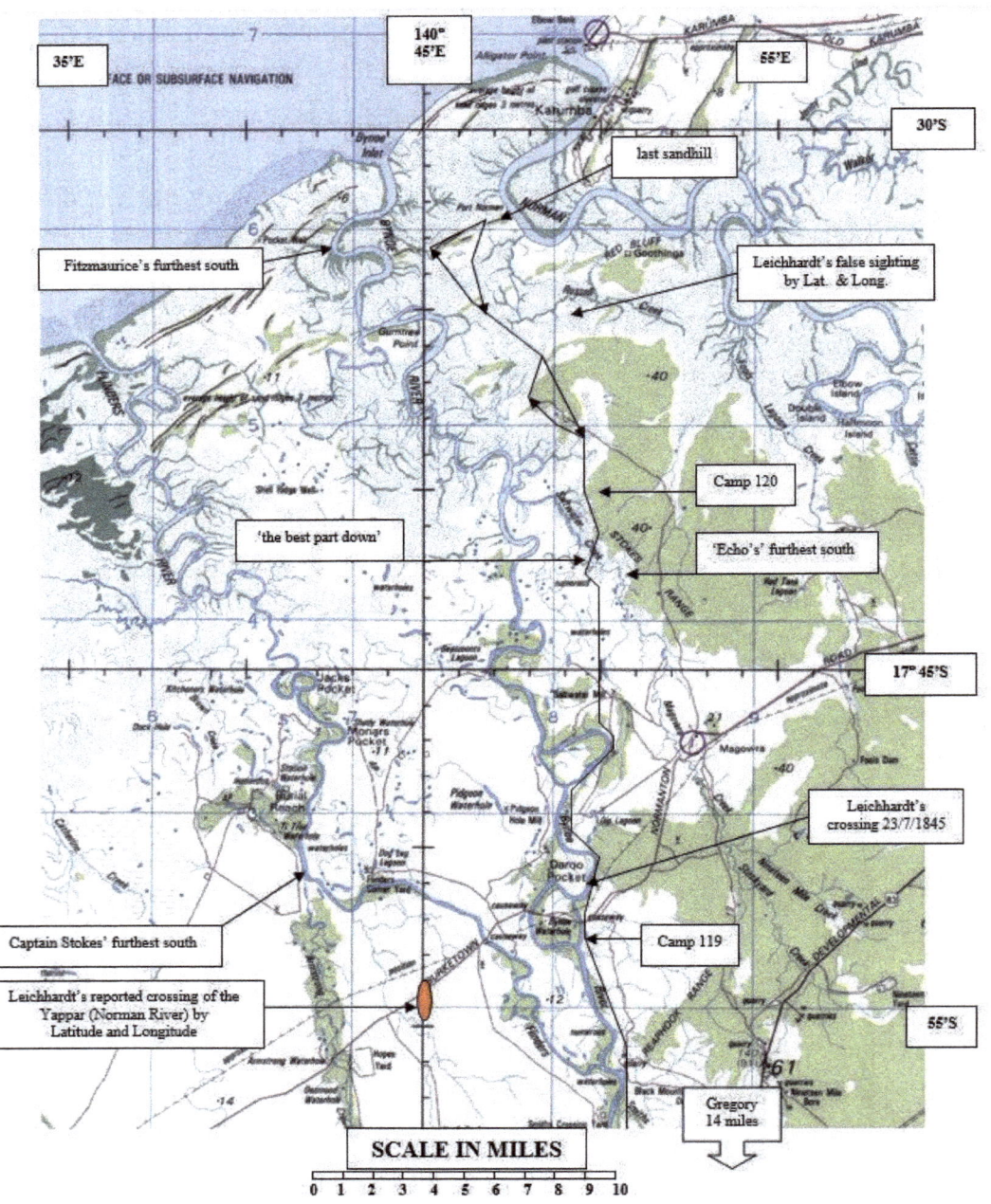

CHAPTER 12: TO THE LAST CAMP

We did much of our research on Magowra Station or travelling to and from there. Early one morning on our way out there, we saw a mob of cattle being herded along the fence next to the road. As a keen photographer, I wanted to take photographs and David, being an obliging driver, pulled up so I could climb on to the top of the 4WD bike on the back of the truck. The stockmen, on horseback, immediately began to show off — cracking their whips and kicking up dust. I got some good photographs and, unbeknown to the stockmen, printed them out on the photo printer that we had in our caravan back in town. The next day I gave them to the station manager, informing him that they were for the stockmen or for blackmail purposes, whichever took his fancy. I have no doubt that he gave them a hard time before handing them the photographs.

Camp 119 Site Today

Camp 119 is marked today by a monument just south of the Burketown Development Road west of Normanton. The camp is two hundred yards to the east of the east bank of the Little Bynoe, just under the edge of the river timber and adjoining a lagoon. It still has the hallmarks of a particularly good campsite if you approach on foot from the south as they would have done. However, the lagoon is only a shadow of its former self having been damaged in the 1974 and 1997 floods.[ii] An old local told us that, prior to 1974, the lagoon was very pretty with many waterlilies, but we saw no sign of them when we were last there.

The lagoon would have looked much like this

The blazed tree that is a feature of the site today is Walker's tree, which was carved on the 12th of January 1862 during his search for Burke and Wills.[iii] It was carved: -

FW
1862

Most of the numerals were still visible on this tree in 1997, but bark has grown back over the others. By measurement of the blazed surface, the tree was only about eight inches in diameter in 1862 and was alive and in good condition when we last saw it with a diameter of about thirteen inches. It has had four major growth periods in its life since Walker, one prior to the end of 1902 when it was found by the staff of Magowra Station nearly grown over[iv], two prior to November 1936[v] and one since, where it attempted unsuccessfully to grow over the blaze in three very good seasons. The Burke and Wills' tree marked **B** and possibly **CXIX** is at a compass bearing of 274° 30' distant one chain 85.5 links (122.43 feet) from Walker's tree. Both Camp 119 and Camp 120 are located on Magowra Station.

This information and a photo of the tree is shown on page 82 and plate 16 of the Queensland Geographical Journal, 25th session, 1909–1910. The photo of the **B** mark appears like the B in a square that Wills recorded on his map for Camp 104. This highlights the possibility that more Burke and Wills' blazed trees may still exist in this northern area and are waiting to be discovered and recorded.

In 1997 other blazed trees from the time that the Burke and Wills party was at Camp 119 still existed; although one of the blazed Burke and Wills trees had disappeared, a victim of the 1974 floods according to a local.[vi] Walker noted another tree blazed with: -

SE. E
14

Walker dug 14 inches, 14 feet and 14 yards[vii] southeast by east and found that the ground had not been disturbed. It should be noted that surveyors in those days usually measured in links (0.66 feet).

In 1909–1910 a survey was done by J. P. Thomson of all the trees blazed at Camp 119 — evidence of how the men occupied themselves during the three days that Burke and Wills pushed north to try to reach the sea. David re-surveyed the area in 1999 — see the plan on the next page.

*By the time we began to take an interest in the site in the mid-1990s, it was in a sad state with visitors driving through the middle of the camp area, leaving rubbish about and even possibly chopping down trees for campfires. Many believe that Walker's tree is the most important on the site and it is certainly the best preserved. The main **B** tree was hidden in the background by an introduced pest: rubber vines. We contacted local service clubs and enlisted their help to cut all the rubber vine down using long ladders and plenty of manpower.*

The next step was involving the Carpentaria Shire Council to tidy up the site. They applied for and received a Regional improvement grant, which enabled them to put up new signage and a shelter. The old signage was, by then, so faded as to be unreadable. The Council used David's information and some of my photographs for the new signage. They also graded a track according to one of David's survey plans of the camp area. As a surveyor and town planner, he was well qualified to carry out this work.

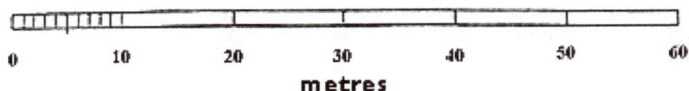
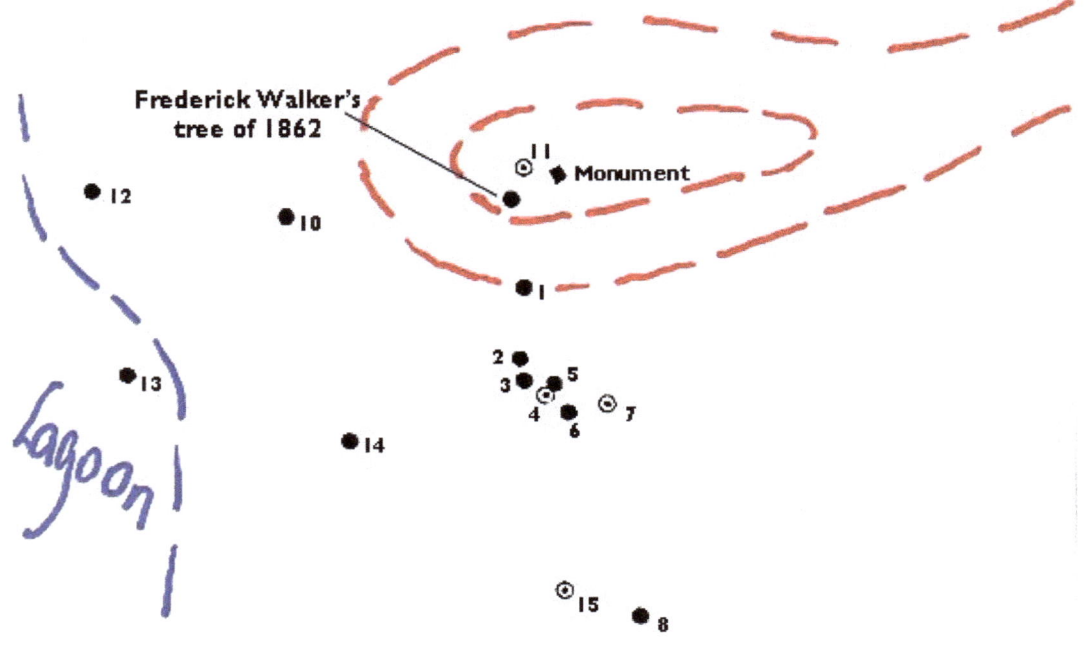

CHAPTER 12: TO THE LAST CAMP

Finally, we prepared an application, supported by the Council, for the site to be Queensland State Heritage listed. (See Appendix 2.)

The site, including the blazed tree from another camp of Walker's some distance away that David had found, was gazetted in 2008 following our application for it to be listed as a State Heritage site of cultural and heritage significance.

We nominated the Council for an award to recognise the work they had done at the site, which they were successful in winning. Below is a photo of the upgraded signage that they put in place. Much of the sign's information is from David's work and the photos in the left background are mine.

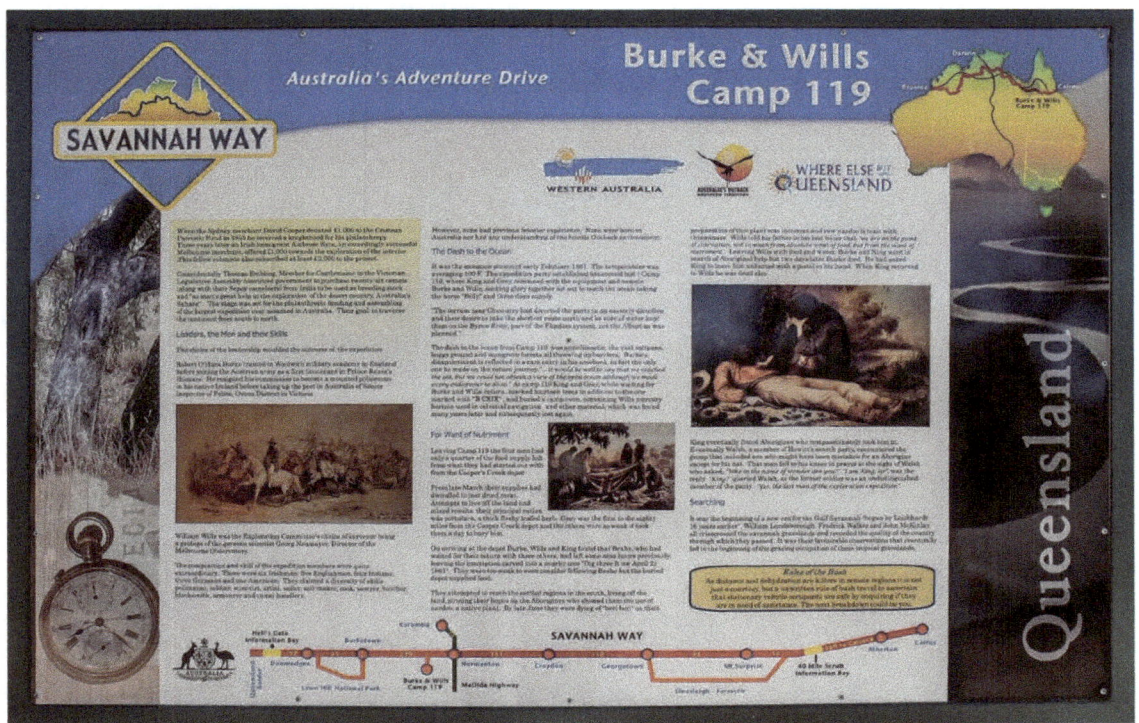

The new signage at Camp 119

Tracking the Trees

Burke and Wills' blazes were not always symmetrical and were not always cut by the same person. They were sometimes half shields, pointed at top and square at the bottom — somewhat like the half shields used by surveyors today. Walker's blazes are full shields, rounded at top and bottom. The tree marked **SE. E 14** should be the subject of further research as it could have been marked by someone else between

Burke and Wills' time and Walker's arrival eleven months later. Macdonald published a copy of his diary about a similar trip where his Camp 16 was in the area just north. Another pioneer pastoralist with the initials **SE** may have been near Burke and Wills' Camp 119 and marked it as his Camp 14, although this is unlikely.

The aforementioned information highlights how clinical and accurate Will's records were — even for the first seven miles of his travels north of Camp 119 along the river. They made no claim of reaching or seeing the sea. Indeed, the record shows a statement from Burke that they did not. If accurate in other instances, why do people dismiss their written record for the 10th of February?

While their daily travelling distances during the previous few weeks ranged from eight to fifteen miles per day or night (they sometimes travelled by moonlight), those distances were accomplished with camels. Since then, few others have seen fit to use camels in this area. A notable exception being Tom Bergin as related in his book.[viii]

I have also tried riding camels in the area, but five hours were quite sufficient, never again. But the area is still daunting to a walker or a person on horseback. The only change since Burke and Wills went through the area is the removal of a negligible proportion of small trees for fence posts. I have walked small sections of their journey along the Flinders in cooler conditions and would not care to match their daily rates achieved in mid-summer. Make no mistake, these were fit men and far from their deathbed at this stage of their journey. Wills' walking abilities in a 48-hour period are on record in proceedings of the Royal Commission from King under oath: -

Qu. 154	Then Mr Wills went out by himself?
King	He went ninety miles; he took McDonough with him and three camels.
Qu. 155	And he lost three of his Camels, did he not?
King	He lost the three and returned on foot.
Qu. 156	Was he much weakened by that Journey?
King	Not Mr. Wills.
Qu. 157	But McDonough was?
King	Rather.
Qu. 158	Did they suffer from want of food as well as want of water?
King	No, only from want of water.[ix]

It would be true to say that Wills, as the person in charge, lost the camels and thus placed the two lives in jeopardy, and this was a foolish mistake. Wills' father pursued this point with quotes from the inquiry: -

> He [Wills] told McDonough that he wished to make some observations, and was going to a rising ground at a distance; that the camels should feed, but he was not to lose sight of them for an instant. Instead of attending to his instructions, McDonough set to work to light a fire and boil his panikin [sic]. Perhaps he went to sleep; for he pointed out some stunted bushes in the distance and said they were the camels. My son then sent him to search for them, but they could not be found. King, the only survivor of the party, on his examination, said: - "Mr Wills told me that the camels were lost through McDonough's neglect during the time he was writing and taking observations.
>
> Qu. 1737   McDonough never disputed that did he?
>
> **King**   McDonough told me that it was while they were at supper in the evening; but I do not see how that could be, because they generally took supper, and ourselves, about six o'clock; and it was so dark they could not see the camels, so that they were most likely lost when Mr. Wills was taking observations. [x]

Beckler described problems with the camels. His notes were written during the period he was travelling with Wright and provide insight into frustrations that explorers faced when travelling with camels: -

> My continual repetition of the animals running away is really very tedious; perhaps one ought to write a separate journal about this. Imagine, though, what a delight it is to wake almost every other morning on an Australian expedition and hear, in addition to all the other difficulties and hindrances, that "the horses are gone" or "the camels are off". This is something that cannot be changed, not even with the greatest care. Luckily, we had enough experience to find the animals even if it sometimes took two days' searching. [xi]

It is good to see that Beckler could retain his sense of humour.

Wills did not record this type of delay in any of his notes north of Coopers Creek and the problem is not reflected in their consistent early starts.

They reasonably assumed that the journey north from 119 would be faster without camels than with them and the rate could be considerably higher when they reached the flatter and clearer country ahead. Their trip north on the 10th was with Billy the horse "with only a saddle and about twenty-five pounds on his back".

We know the horse carried: -

> at least two pistols,[xii] estimate total five pounds.
> hobbles for horse, estimate two pounds.
> three days' provisions.

They probably each had their wet weather gear comprising one piece of oilcloth, weight 4 pounds, plus one poncho, weight 8 pounds, i.e., 12 pounds (about 5.5 kilograms) each with the ponchos carried personally.

We can only speculate on what the remaining provisions might have been.

Wills would have had his compass and telescope, plus minor utensils. Did they carry an axe and chisel for marking trees or even a "tomahawk" (a quantity of these were in their original supplies)? [xiii] They had marked many campsites without entering the fact in the diary. Blazing trees at campsites appeared to be a formality although, in his diary, Beckler recorded many unmarked campsites[xiv] as they tried to follow Burke and Wills' route northward. Was the practice to continue? Did they plan to mark a tree when they reached the coast? Could they afford the weight penalty or the time on this final dash?

The fact that so many trees were blazed at Camp 119 suggests that an axe may have been left there, where greater use could be made of it. Did the Expedition have two? Could they afford the weight penalty and luxury of two for the whole Expedition? Was it within their policy of carrying spares? Was King's above-mentioned statement correct? Cutting a number or letter on a tree, unless it is similar to a 1 or an X, is extremely difficult with an axe. The preferred instrument is a chisel, while a knife is useful only on a small-dimensioned sapling. A branding iron could also be used but it would probably not create an enduring mark and would be added weight to carry.

Burke and Wills may have marked a tree from Camp 102 with an axe. The mark is of roman numerals, which are generally easier to cut with an axe. The tree in questions is preserved outside the Library in Cloncurry and was supposedly taken from the Corella Riverbank, but locals have some suspicion as to its authenticity. The marking of the **BW** is suspect as the Expedition was not known as the Burke and Wills Expedition until later. They marked a tree two campsites later with a **B** in a box, so why the change? This **BW** marking bears no similarity to the **B** at Camp 119, photographed in 1909.

Blazed tree at Camp 119

To blaze a tree, numbers are not cut into the bark. The bark is first removed as a "shield" usually with an axe, and then numbers are cut into the bare timber. The bark can, in time, grow back over the numbers. After it has grown completely over, one can remove the "shield" by cutting around the edge with an axe, then giving the shield a couple of hits with the back of the axe. The shield will pop off, often with a complete negative of the original markings. An example of this is displayed in the Adelaide Offices of the Royal Geographical Society of South Australia located within the State Library on North Terrace.

An example of the reverse of a shield, photo by Richard Cork

Exceptions to this growth pattern are the "bottle" trees in northern Australia. With these trees, the same bark stays with the tree and stretches. Augustus Gregory's tree just downstream of Timber Creek is a well-known example and is open to tourists. Another exception is the palm tree.

Explorers and surveyors often have "signature blazes" although current surveyors must comply with survey regulations for marking trees on roads, corners and boundaries.

A relatively new blaze made by the Main Roads Department

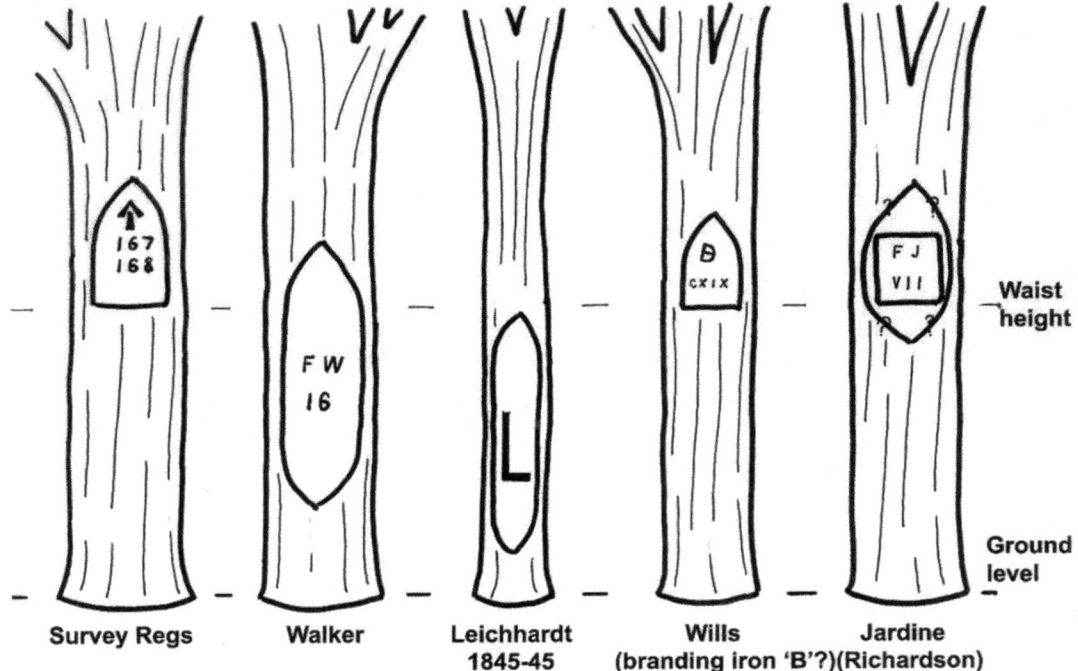

EXPLORERS' TREE MARKS - THEIR SIGNATURES David Hillan 2004

Matching Wills' Notes Upstream

The first few miles of their trip north along the riverbank from Camp 119 was confirmed by Walker in his 1862 search.

Let us walk in Wills' shoes for this trip north: -

> Sunday, February 1861. Finding the ground in such a state from the heavy falls of rain, that camels could scarcely get along, it was decided to leave them at camp 119, and Mr. Burke and I to proceed towards the sea on foot. After breakfast we accordingly started, taking with us the horse and three days' provisions. Our first difficulty was in crossing Billy's Creek, which we had to do where it enters the river, a few hundred yards below the camp. In getting the horse in here he got bogged in a quicksand bank so deeply as to be unable to stir, and we only succeeded in extricating him by undermining him on the creek's side, and then lugging him in the water. [xv]

CHAPTER 12: TO THE LAST CAMP

The area one mile south of Camp 119 contains many steep-sided creeks that would be difficult to cross in wet weather — they are bad enough in the dry. Billy's Creek, a short distance north of Camp 119, is a double creek that joins at the river's bank with a high bank on the northern side.

> Having got all the things in safety, we continued down the riverbank, which bent about from east to west, but kept a general north course. A great deal of the land was so soft and rotten that the horse, with only a saddle and about twenty-five pounds on his back, could scarcely walk over it.

At less than two miles, they were further north than John Lort Stokes' most southerly point on the Flinders River, which was 8.5 miles to the west. They thought they were on the same river, not the Bynoe which was their actual location, and would have believed they were close to the most southerly point that Stokes had reached. At less than four miles they unknowingly crossed Leichhardt's actual route.

> At a distance of about five miles we again had him bogged in crossing a small creek, after which he seemed so weak that we had great doubts about getting him on. We, however, found some better ground close to the water's edge, where the sandstone rock crops out, and we struck to it as far as possible. Finding the river was bending about so much that we were making very little progress in a northerly direction, we struck off due north. [xvi]

Looking at the AUSLIG map (see page 106), we can understand their concern. Parts of the river were heading north-northeast, making their journey to the coast longer. North or north-northwest would have been their preference. We can identify the point of their direction change within a couple of hundred yards. They would have turned north within two hundred yards of latitude 17° 46' 40", longitude 140° 49' 50". This is approximately three miles west of the current Magowra homestead. We know this as their notes state that they were following the river and had just worked around a change in river direction of 170° — this would have directed them southwest, away from their goal. The AUSLIG map and air photos show they were at a point where they could see the river heading nearly southwest for two miles. They had no reason to abandon the river before this point, while it was still going mainly north.

Wills continues: -

> and soon came on some table-land, where the soil is shallow and gravelly, and clothed with box and swamp gums. [xvii]

The concept of tableland was hard for me to grasp in the context of such flat plains. Especially as I had grown up and worked in more undulating country; it misled me for some time. If the definition of a tableland is accepted as a flat piece of country with the water draining away in every direction, then Wills' description was accurate, even though the height of the tableland may have been negligible.

They were on the lower flood plain of the Bynoe for the whole day.

Wills continues: -

> Patches of the land were very boggy, but the main portion was sound enough; beyond this we came to an open plain, covered with water up to one's ankles. The soil here was a stiff clay, and the surface very uneven, so that between the tufts of grass one was frequently knee deep in water. The bottom, however, was sound and no fear of bogging.
>
> After floundering through this for several miles, we came to a path formed by the blacks, and there were distinct signs of a recent migration in a southerly direction.

Was the season just about to change?

> By making use of this path we got on much better, for the ground was well trodden and hard. At rather more than a mile, the path entered a forest through which flowed a nice watercourse, and we had not got far before we found places where the blacks had been camping.

This does not show up on the AUSLIG maps as the detail is too fine. However, the stereoscopic view from a pair of overlapping air photos shows the micro creek pattern in detail, confirming Wills' description.

We always travelled to the Gulf country in far north Queensland in winter, which was the dry season — known locally as The Dry. This made the necessary field research easier for us to do. We miscalculated only twice. All the brochures claimed that it never rained in the Gulf country in May. Once, after fishing all day, the rain poured down as we returned to the Karumba boat ramp and continued while we cleaned the fish. At that time, we were camping in a tent and cooking outside on a small gas stove. The gas ran out and we looked at each other, dripping wet, and decided not to go into the tent to change. Instead, we took ourselves off to the local hotel for a meal in the Suave Bar (there were two bars — the other was the Animal Bar, need I say more?). At about 10pm after a pleasant meal accompanied by nice wine, we looked out the window to see the

CHAPTER 12: TO THE LAST CAMP

rain still falling heavily so we decided to get a room in the adjacent motel. The next morning, when we returned to the caravan park still in our wet clothes, the other residents naturally took advantage of the opportunity to make remarks.

In another year we left the van home and took swags, which turned out not to be the best alternative. That June was the coldest on record in far north Queensland. In the middle of the night, I heard the motor of the truck start and went out to find David huddled up in the cabin with the heaters running. Naturally, I joined him for the rest of the night — not the most comfortable night's sleep I have ever had, but at least it was a bit warmer than the swags.

Wills continues: -

> The forest was intersected by little pebbly rises, on which they had made their fires, and in the sandy ground adjoining some of the former had been digging yams, which seemed to be so numerous that they could afford to leave lots of them about, probably having only selected the very best.
>
> We were not so particular, but ate many of those that they had rejected, and found them very good. About half a mile further, we came close on a black fellow, who was coiling up by a campfire, whilst his gin and piccaninny were yabbering alongside. We stopped for a short time to take out some of the pistols that were on the horse, and that they might see us before we were so near as to frighten them. Just as we stopped, the black got up to stretch his limbs, and after a few seconds looked in our direction. It was very amusing to see the way in which he stared, standing for some time as if he thought he must be dreaming, and then, having signalled to the others, they dropped on their haunches, and shuffled off in the quietest manner possible. Near their fire was a fine hut, the best I have ever seen, built on the same principle as those at Cooper's Creek, but much larger and more complete: I should say a dozen blacks might comfortably coil in it together.

While he mentioned some intermediate mileage, he did not give a running log of distances, which makes interpretation difficult.

Wills continues: -

> It is situated at the end of the forest towards the north, and looks out on an extensive marsh, which is at times flooded by seawater.

> Hundreds of wild geese, plover and pelicans, were enjoying themselves in the watercourses on the marsh, all the water on which was too brackish to be drinkable, except some holes that are filled by the stream that flows through the forest. The neighbourhood of this encampment is one of the prettiest we have seen during the journey. Proceeding on our course across the marsh, we came to a channel through which the sea water enters. Here we passed three blacks, who, as is universally their custom, pointed out to us, unasked, the best part down. This assisted us greatly, for the ground we were taking was very boggy. [xviii]

This is the first time Wills' mentions sea water. Saltwater Creek is the most southerly place where mangroves exist as shown on the AUSLIG MAGOWRA 1:100,000. I have attempted to check this with satellite imaging, but the expense is beyond my resources. However, AUSLIG's records confirm that the limit of the mangroves on the MAGOWRA sheet is correct. These air photos confirm that this point is the first contact with the northern saline flats. This would have been their first view of the Stokes Range's high ground due north and to the east. Judging from the AUSLIG map, and more particularly the air photos, Wills provided a good description of Saltwater Creek just upstream from its junction with a westerly creek at latitude 17° 41' 50" where it then changes course from approximately north–south to an east–west direction.

I agree with Wills' description of the marsh being extensive, but it was small compared with what he would see the next day near noon. He made no reference to the tidal height change though he did mention that this creek was tidal. A tidal range of 2.4 metres (7 feet and 10.5 inches) is mentioned in a brief Burke and Wills summary[xix]; however, the source is not quoted. The only original reference regarding tidal height change that I have found is from King's casual observations at Camp 119, mentioned during the Commission.

I am puzzled by this as I found no evidence in the vegetation or taste of the water that the river is tidal at Camp 119. Such evidence is also not found below the causeway that now exists, about a mile downstream. However, I have not been in the area when the tides are more than 3.3 metres, and the February of 1861 when Burke and Wills were there tides were approaching 4 metres. Perhaps such evidence does exist at Camp 119 when the tide is that high.

Camp 119 is about twenty river miles upstream from the last of the mangroves shown on AUSLIG's map. The riverbed would rise more than seventy centimetres over the twenty miles, which would be the top limit of a king tide at four metres.

Having said that, I have seen saltwater crocodiles in the Flinders River due west of Camp 119 and also crocodiles in the Flinders 20 miles further south (i.e. upstream of the Bynoe branch off), although I could not confirm whether they were salt or freshwater crocodiles.

Crossing Saltwater Creek

I have taken my 16-foot boat, Echo, up Saltwater Creek to latitude 17º 42' 08", longitude 140º 50' 28" on a tide at 3.29 meters. High tide there was about two and a halfhours later than Karumba. At this point the creek has completed its east–west course towards the Stokes Range and then changes direction to generally due south. At that time the creek was still lined with some mangroves and was about thirty feetwide at its maximum.

No further access was possible in my craft and turning around in the rapidly running tide was difficult. The tide was at its maximum, about to change, but was still running in fast. River tides are greatly affected by the volume of water and cross section of the stream. It is not the slow and imperceptible change of a beach tide.

In such circumstances, one risks becoming trapped in a boat in a matter of minutes. This east–west section is where Burke and Wills most probably crossed Saltwater Creek. If they had travelled exactly due north from their river turn-off point, they would have reached the centre of this east–west section. The AUSLIG map shows that section as a swamp and old river loop. From a topography point of view, they would probably have been west of the centre of that river loop. The AUSLIG map indicates only two possible approaches from the south when wet conditions prevail.

No rock bar exists at latitude 17° 42' 07", longitude 140° 49' 27", although a low sand ridge from the south joins the creek on a bend. Here the water depth was a maximum of 1.5 metres on my depth sounder at a tide height of 3.29 metres. It was above a zero-level tide by at least 1.79 metres, meaning any water above the sand ridge had to be freshwater, unless seawater remained trapped from a previous high tide. At this point, the creek was about forty-five feet wide and as you go upstream (towards the south) the water deepens to two metres again. The mangroves thin out and freshwater tree species start to appear on the banks. Both of these types of trees are easy to walk through.

The sand ridge reaches the creek on a bend and is about three feet higher than the surrounding country. If you crossed, you would find yourself arriving on the inside of the river's bend with a gently sloping shore running down to the water level — in contrast to the rest of the river's customary vertical three to four feet drop. Short vegetation covers the shoreline to the water's edge and when I visited, I happened upon two Brolgas browsing through the greenery. I had never seen this gentle incline and vegetation in these creek systems before.

Crocodiles are a most primitive reptile and have survived like no other form of animal life. They have not achieved this by taking risks; they hunt and fight on their own terms. While I have seen them cross beaches and sand up to one hundred yards wide, they typically hunt at close quarters in deeper water within four to five yards of cover. All crocodiles that we have seen on riverbanks confirmed this pattern. The sand ridge crossing described here does not have a large waterhole with a small tidal heavily mangrove-overgrown side creek suitable to hide a crocodile at lower tide levels. This would have been recognized by Aboriginal Peoples who have coexisted with these reptiles for centuries.

Stokes made various comments on crocodiles that he observed: -

> Alligators being so very numerous I was surprised to notice what little dread the natives appeared to have of them, dancing and wading about in the water near the bank, as if they and the animal had entered into a treaty of amity. [xx]

The Aboriginal Peoples' knowledge of crocodiles would have been far more detailed than that of Stokes.

If I had to cross the creek in this area and avoid crocodiles, this is the only point that I would consider. It is also the only place a horse could easily approach the creek. Surely this must be the "best part down" shown to Burke and Wills by the local Aboriginal People who were at the time migrating south?

When Burke and Wills arrived at this east–west section of Saltwater Creek, most likely late in the afternoon, the water would have been about a hundred and forty centimetres lower than when we visited on my boat.

I have flown over this east–west section of the creek when the tide height was 1.4 metres but only momentarily spotted one point of low water as the helicopter swung around. This must have been the place where my boat's sounder had shown a depth of 1.5 metres. I decided to check it out on the ground later via helicopter, which was the only form of access at low tide. We chose to investigate at a 1.71 metres flat dodge tide of several hours to maximize accuracy. We had to wait eight days to achieve this.

Saltwater Creek at low tide

This visit confirmed the information from the boat's sounder. The scale can be judged by the two people dressed in red and blue halfway up the left bank in the above photograph.

At this point on the bend, the deepest section lies to the outer three yards with a gradual slope upwards to the middle of the bend. This shallow section is about one hundred and fifty yards long. The photographs and levels show conclusively that Burke and Wills' and the local Aboriginal People's creek crossing must have been at this point. Therefore, we can unquestionably identify this as the "best part down" shown to them by the Aboriginal People.

Our boat Echo at the same point on Saltwater Creek at high tide

According to the current state of this crossing, they would have been up to their ankles on the way north and above their knees on the way south. But perhaps the water was shallower in their times. When I visited, I noted with surprise that the sandy bottom had no hazardous debris threatening a would-be crosser. Currents continually scour this sandy ridge, so much that it resembles the bottom of a bathtub rather than a bush creek (which could explain why I have never seen professional mud crab fishermen operating in this creek though I have seen them in most others.) This suggests that the bottom is much lower now than in Burke and Wills' time and, with no evidence of sunken logs, the crossing could have been even easier in 1861 than it is today.

The tide chart shows that in February the river reaches a low tide level on all but five days. On those five days, tides are only another 0.5 metres higher, so February would be a reliable month for Aboriginal People to cross on a daily basis. Wills' diary also noted the dry weather while they were travelling down the river system. Some rain had fallen during the preceding week,[xxi] but not enough to prevent Wills from completing his full latitude and longitude observations each day.

Their only comments about being slowed on their journey was briefly one morning at Camp 119 and for several days about a week later. Examining Wills' distance estimates between camps on the way north revealed they were also slowed between Camps 118 and 119. Perhaps this was due to rain; however, this section is rough country with a lot of steep creeks and the 119 campsite is a special one. Therefore, I do not believe that the creek was unduly flooded at the time Burke and Wills crossed. Even if it was, I know from experience that surveyors carry out creek crossings with water up to their chins and at times they have to swim.

Stokes certainly followed that practice: -

> I had stripped to swim across a creek... when an alligator rose close by... My only chance of escaping the monster was to hasten back to the boat, and to cross the last creek before the alligator, who appeared fully aware of my intentions. It was now, therefore, a mere matter of speed between us, and the race began. I started off with the utmost rapidity, the alligator keeping pace with me in the water. After a sharp and anxious race, I reached the last creek, which was now much swollen; while the difficulty of crossing was aggravated by my desire to save my gun. Plunging in I reached the opposite shore just in time to see the huge jaws of the alligator extended close above the spot where I had quitted the water.[xxii]

He could not refrain from shuddering as he sat down to regain his breath. He did not mention if the incident had any effect on his ability to sleep that night.

Surveyors are not the only ones to risk deep waters. The rock bar downstream from Borroloola at the Fishing Club on the McArthur River is the site of a local story about Aboriginal People using it as a crossing at low tide. With water up to their necks, they proceeded in a special order designed so that the most important members of the tribe would survive a crocodile attack. That probably meant that they sent the old women across first! Stockmen, in the early days, would swim cattle out to the Wellesley Islands northwest of the Bynoe on low tide.[xxiii] Even in recent years people ignore the threat from crocodiles at creek crossings.

One documented crocodile incident involved bushman Les Henry who served the local Normanton community as Shire Chairman for seventeen years. He was riding and swimming his horse across a creek when, without warning, a huge crocodile surfaced and grabbed it by the head. Two days later Henry went back, found the body of the horse minus the head; however, he was able to retrieve his saddle. He used to complain that he lost his bridle.[xxiv]

The curator of the Survey museum in Brisbane tells a related story from records of a north Queensland surveyor named Alfred Starcke early last century: -

> He would add fifty percent to his account if the water was up to his knees and the crocs were three feet long. The surcharge was one hundred percent if they were six feet long and the water up to his arse.

The Surveyor General reprimanded Starcke, telling him: -

> he must use courteous language in official correspondence.

Starcke replied: -

> I presume you refer to my use of the word "arse". If you will look in Webster's Dictionary you will find that it means "the buttocks of a Man".

I detect the frustration and lack of sleep in a surveyor whose mosquito-filled nights were spent on longhand calculations by the light of a candle or oil lamp. The old Lands Department Regulation book from 1914 that I have in my collection states that the rates then were either "sixpence or nine pence a chain [66 feet]" with provision for "local increase". I would certainly classify the presence of crocodiles and the wading depth of the water as a justifiable local increase. Indeed, I think the percentage claimed was a bit on the conservative side.

A creek crossing certainly does not have to be a dry shoe one

Burke and Wills made no mention of crocodiles and other explorers only mentioned them occasionally but generally without the fears expressed today. Thus, I am confident that they crossed the creek successfully at this point.

We can reasonably assume that they crossed at the shallowest point, which certainly would have had attributes that set it apart. According to current weather calculations, the season would have been just beginning to change but was not yet as wet as it would be. In fact, five days later, it started pouring and continued to do so for six days, halting their southward journey — time that they could not afford to lose (Camps 4R to 10R equals Camps 114, 115, 116). They lost four days here to rain. This time loss increased as they headed further south.

The following Wet season, when Walker was in the area, was certainly a wet one. He made multiple crossings of the Saltwater/Magowra Creek about four miles south (upstream) from Burke and Wills' crossing point. On the 1st of January 1862, Walker also recorded meeting an "old black" during his trip north at a point that would have been four or five miles south of his crossing point.

Walker detoured east because of flooding in the creek. He crossed the creek higher upstream, then proceeded north through boggy conditions along the western section of the Stokes Range adjoining Saltwater and Magowra creeks. When he reached the edge of the saltwater inlet "our old black was here again".[xxv] Obviously he had made good progress on a track known to him, possibly even crossing at the same "best part down" point as Burke and Wills. Local knowledge was certainly an advantage.

Burke and Wills crossed Saltwater Creek, a fact that some people do not believe. Often, they suggest that the pair followed Saltwater Creek down its west bank and were trapped, but this theory does not allow for Walker's findings. I believe five additional factors support their crossing.

1. With their experience of following rivers downstream, Burke and Wills would be aware that tributaries had to be crossed either immediately or further upstream. A downstream crossing would be more difficult or impossible due to increasing width and depth. (Both Leichhardt and Walker followed this practice).

> July 23, When Charley returned this morning with the horses, he told me, that a fine broad saltwater river was before us. I kept, therefore, at once to the southward, and feared that I should have to go far in that direction before being able to ford it. After travelling about two miles, we came in sight of it. It was broad and deep, with low rocky banks... We had travelled, however, more than a mile on its bank, when we came to a broad rocky barrier or dam extending across the river, over which a small stream of brackish water rippled, and, by means of this, we

crossed without difficulty. I now steered again north-west by west. [xxvi]

2. This was also Leichhardt's crossing of the Bynoe just north of Camp 119 and it casts doubts on King's tide sightings at Camp 119. Burke and Wills could see high ground to their east and stretching right around through the northeast to due north. They would have sought to reach that area as soon as possible, even with a slight direction change, to ensure drier travelling and to gain distant views, which would confirm that they were still in touch with the river. They would not turn away from that opportunity. If they were not following Leichhardt's reported sea sighting, then their decision to travel due north from the bend in the Bynoe was a dangerous gamble. They were short of time.

3. Burke and Wills would know to avoid the mangroves due to entrapment possibilities and lack of a line of sight ahead. They would not turn towards them.

4. If they followed the creek downstream, they would have had to make a very difficult crossing of Saltwater Creek, west arm.

5. Wills stated in his final letter to his father, written a few days before his death, that they had "a successful trip to Carpentaria and back".[xxvii]

Saltwater Creek at this point is tidal and they recognised that as previously mentioned. The tidal level would have been about four feet six inches lower on their return. See Tide Charts (next page) and note the time difference at the Bynoe River.

Due to the scouring I noted along the bottom of the creek, we can reasonably deduce that the bottom of the creek would have been at a higher level in 1861, i.e., the crossing depth would have been less. Wills' next entry states: "We moved slowly down about three miles and then camped for the night; the horse Billy being completely baked."[xxviii]

CHAPTER 12: TO THE LAST CAMP

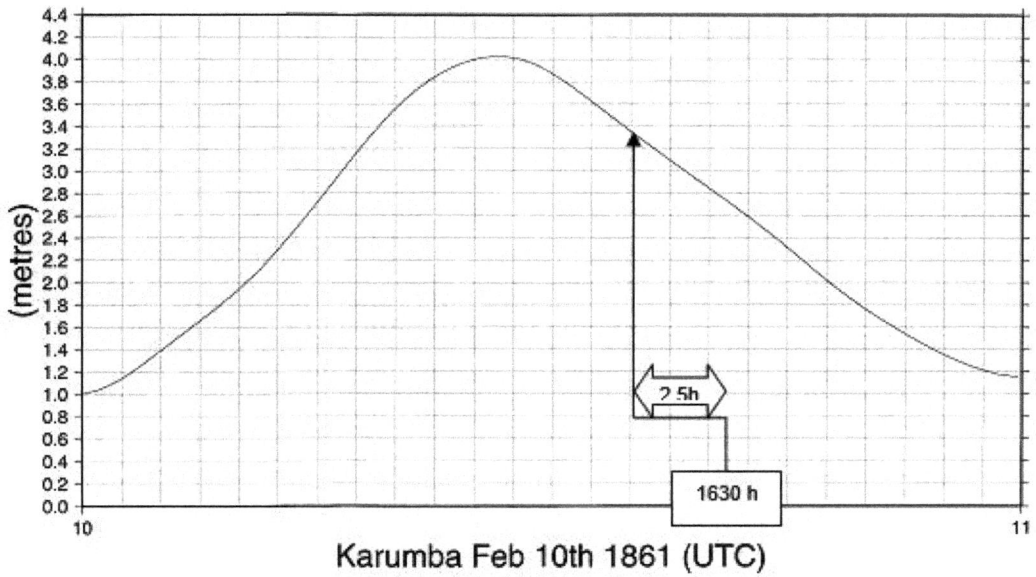

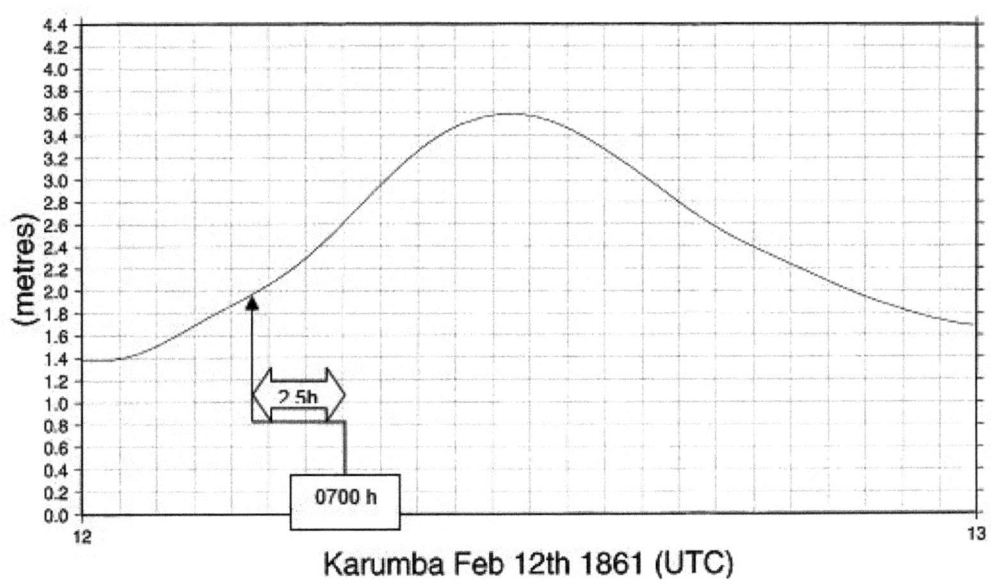

CHAPTER 13
THE LAST CAMP

Understanding why campsites are chosen explains the camping choices of Burke and Wills. They did not just camp at a predetermined time. A campsite had to have certain features, and these were not readily available every few hundred yards. Therefore, if they came to a good site before their planned finishing time for the day, then they would take it.

Camp 119 is a good example of this. As you approach from the myriad of southern creek crossings, its good features are evident. Before the 1974 floods it was a lovely waterlily filled freshwater billabong with a good flat camping area and grass for the horse.

No similar site exists anywhere nearby. This is perhaps why the distance between Camp 118 and Camp 119 is shorter than might be expected. Even today, people camping with a four-wheel drive or a caravan carefully choose their campsites in this way. Campers take a lot of trouble to choose a campsite that meets their needs.

Never camped? Consider how fussy you are about choosing a suburb, a street or a house to live in.

The caravan pictured on the next page was only the second to reach Rutland Plains Station on the western side of Cape York. And, according to the surprised manager, just the first to leave.

Before travelling on the Chillagoe Road (this time in search of Ludwig Leichhardt), we had asked some Normanton locals about the condition of the road. One said, "She's good mate, she's good" while another said, "She's bad mate, she's bad." As it turned out, both were right. Some sections were horrible and others quite good. We did about $2000 worth of damage to our van. We certainly made sure that next time we had the right mobile home for the terrain.

CHAPTER 13: THE LAST CAMP

Finally, we had learned our lesson and returned home to buy a small off-road van — much more suitable for the roads and tracks in far north Queensland

The only problem we found with the little T-van was when we were travelling along a dirt track and I looked in the rear vision mirror to see cutlery flying out from the side of the van in all directions.

I confess — it was my fault. I had neglected to lock the pull-out kitchen drawer after a stop for a cup of tea.

The T-van set up for camp on a carefully chosen spot in the middle of nowhere

Air photo stereo modelling shows that the journey north of Camp 119 was an interesting section. It probably featured some of the clearest travelling that they had experienced for a long time.

The AUSLIG photos of the area showed a "beach" at the top of the river's periodic flood plain, just below the six or seven metre cliffs at the western side of the Stokes Range. (See next page.)

Ridge above the probable location of Camp 120

Burke and Wills would have reached this "beach" after travelling about three quarters of a mile across the marsh, heading northeast towards the escarpment. The escarpment would have been an irresistible magnet because of its height, which enabled views forward and much drier travelling.

The "beach" then headed north-northwest but this direction shift would not have concerned them. They would still be following the river and would remain just clear of the mangroves that adjoined their path to the west. It suited their needs perfectly. For approximately the next two miles, the "beach" wanders in and out slightly. Thus, at the change in direction at 3 miles, a direct advance north of 2.6 miles had been made. Wills himself recorded "about three miles" of walking,[i] which matches the actual distance according to current maps. His estimate is indisputably correct.

I have viewed the whole of this section in a helicopter at low level on two separate occasions. I have walked south and then north along this section of the "beach" for over a mile at its northern end. Not once did I see anything that remotely resembled a site where you could camp for the night, bearing in mind the need for water, feed and security for the horse. It was bleak. The "beach" stands out clearly like a well-defined track.

This is a helicopter used for mustering

The long-suffering wife was lucky enough to fly in this helicopter during mustering (with her camera). Often the pilots of these helicopters were stockmen who usually rode horses. Some of them tended to fly helicopters as if they were still on horseback, making an interesting ride for the passenger — and, occasionally, nausea. Fortunately for me, my many years at sea had fortified my stomach.

I noticed while walking in the area that the stock hoofprints from the previous season were about six inches deep, both above and below the "beach". In contrast, on the "beach," none was evident indicating that "beach" walking was easier in wet conditions. This would explain why Frederick Walker did not find more tracks of the horse Billy or footprints of Burke and Wills.

Walker commented: -

> we had to lead our horses to the edge of a saltwater inlet, now however fresh, where the sands gave the horses good footing. [ii]

Nowadays, when walking in the area in dry conditions one tends to walk on the "beach" where the footing is firm, not on the slightly soft sandy flats that surround. I found myself following it as a matter of course and walked along it for several miles in different places. I have no doubt that Burke and Wills would have discovered this quickly in the wet season. They would surely have headed towards the escarpment as soon as possible after they crossed Saltwater creek. From the crossing to the escarpment would have been tough walking that mirrored their approach to the creek, but the remaining section would have been much easier. I have walked nearly half of that section.

The Ideal Camp Site

The stereo air photo modelling shows that, at the change in direction point at about three miles, the cliffs turn in to form two half amphitheatres. (See below.)

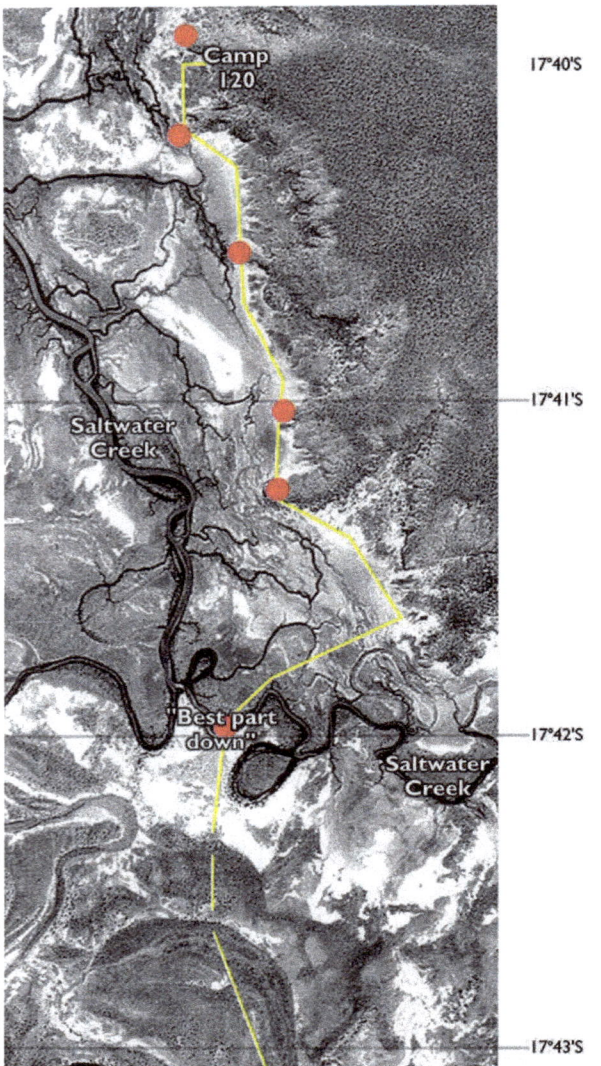
Route between Camps 119 and 120

The first one has a radius of about fifty yards and the second one a radius of one hundred and forty yards and they both generally run north-northeast. These cliffs run north for one hundred and eighty yards, then due east for several hundred yards and then change to a north-northeast direction up a valley of about four miles.

On the western side of these two amphitheatres is a lagoon about half a mile long in the dry season, but much longer in the Wet. This would have left just a narrow rocky entrance to the first amphitheatre, about eight yards wide. The lagoon features a type of mangrove and a type of bulrush that thrive in less salinity than the tidal creeks. In the early Wet, the water is likely fresh with its salinity rising later in the dry season. This lagoon in the Wet could be the one Walker described and the one he, on first sighting, mistook for the river.

The first amphitheatre is not suitable for camping due to a rocky floor and a lack of feed, as well as leaving them exposed to potential attack from the 30 foot cliffs. Coupled with that, any Aboriginal Peoples walking north or south would be forced to walk through the camp, so they could not safely leave the horse there unattended for the day. This was a problem as depicted in the woodcut of John Lort Stokes' spearing shown on page 96.

The second, larger amphitheatre met all their requirements for a good campsite. It has a freshwater creek nearby that flows at that time of the year, grass above the "beach", shade and a secluded place near the water for the horse to be left short hobbled. Their campsite would have been clear of the cliffs for these safety reasons. Around midday that day, they had unpacked their pistols, indicating their caution.[iii]

Without these features, a horse could not have been left alone for the day. Horses can be hobbled. However, short hobbling (i.e., moving the straps inwards over the five links in the hobble chain), really confines the horse. This practice is seldom used without close proximity of water, food, shade and seclusion. Burke and Wills chose to short hobble Billy while they headed further north. The unique site with all these features was a fortuitous find that could not have been planned.

Walker crossed Saltwater/Magowra Creek on the 1st of January 1862, in a wetter season, about four miles upstream (south) from Burke and Wills' crossing. He also made several similar crossings over the next few days. His camp was at latitude 17º 48' near the Bynoe. On the 3rd of January, Walker relocated north about thirteen miles to an area that he had already partly explored. He described the western edge of the Stokes Range with its "deep sharp point round which the river runs".[iv] The thirteen miles of his indirect route corresponds roughly with the twin amphitheatres. His tracker, Jingle, found a Burke and Wills campfire site but no marked trees. Walker did not record marking one either, though he did at other camps. Another of his party noticed horse tracks[v] on the 4th. We do not have enough information to tie the campfire and horse track sightings to a specific point, but the general area was probably in the northwest corner of the range, east of Saltwater Creek.

Walker reported that at his campsite in this area, less than a year after Burke and Wills: -

> The mosquitoes were intolerable at night and the poor horses kept under the smoke, which we kept up all night. [vi]

When you consider daily temperatures of around 100° Fahrenheit (about 40° Celsius), the extremely high humidity and the amount of fresh rainwater around to breed mosquitoes, you can imagine how uncomfortable it must have been to try and sleep. It seems unreasonable to sleep beside a fire in such conditions. However, I have myself been forced into the same situation. While the temperature is higher near the fire, the humidity is lower, there are fewer mosquitoes and you do get a slightly better night's rest. I am not surprised that the horses had worked that out.

Stokes records: -

> I must be pardoned for again alluding to our old enemies the musquitoes [sic], but the reception they gave us this night is too deeply engraven [sic] on my memory to be ever quite forgotten. They swarmed around us, and by the light of the fire, the blanket bags in which the men sought to protect themselves, seemed literally black with the crawling and stinging persecutors. Woe to the

unhappy wretch who had left unclosed the least hole in his bag; the persevering musquitoes surely found it out, and as surely drove the luckless occupant out of his retreat. I noticed one man dressed as if in the frozen north, hold his bag over the fire till it was quite full of smoke, and then get into it, a companion securing the mouth over his head at the apparent risk of suffocation; he obtained three hours of what he gratefully termed comfortable sleep, but when he emerged from his shelter, where he had been stewed up with the thermometer at 87°, his appearance may be easily be imagined... One poor fellow, whose patience was quite exhausted, fairly jumped into the river to escape further persecution. [vii]

Flinders retained his sense of humour in similar circumstances when he noted: -

One of these vallies [sic] at the south end of Cotton's Island, might be made a delightful situation to a college of monks, who could bear the heat of the climate, and were impenetrable to the stings of musketoes [sic]. [viii]

These comments reflect the morale, the conditions, their practice and their equipment which is not directly recorded elsewhere in their notes. Burke and Wills would have camped under identical conditions to Walker.

A Closer Inspection — Visiting the Area

I decided to check the general area of their last camp north, Camp 120, on the ground. The only available and practical way to visit the site at the time was by water; a return journey of about seventy miles from Karumba, which was the nearest launching point.

Identifying the best tie-up point along Saltwater Creek required careful air photo interpretation so that we would not be trapped by the mangroves. It was difficult to find a point that offered disembarkation through the mangroves and a safe place to moor in a rapid tide change. We noticed such a site just as we went past and, as I turned the boat at latitude 17° 40' 07", longitude 140° 48' 43" in close confines, a Pheasant Coucal flew out of the exact spot where I planned to moor. It was the only one seen that season. As it flew over the creek I thought "doesn't it look scrawny?"

Wills must really be getting to me.

CHAPTER 13: THE LAST CAMP

Our boat, Echo, tied up in Saltwater Creek

Recording the position of our boat on our handheld GPS was important from a safety point of view. The gap in the mangroves at the entrance to a small creek was only about ten feet wide with a small, very shy, resident crocodile.

After the craft was tied up, it was invisible from the land at fifty yards away on an incoming tide — despite being coloured safety yellow on the hull with a yellow canopy on a white superstructure. Therefore, we took care to carry a GPS and very great care to identify which pair of mangrove fingers we had walked out from. In the next photo, the boat is invisible.

The long-suffering wife hauling the bag of concrete and tools for the C120 monument

The centre of the larger amphitheatre is fourteen and half miles north in a direct line from Camp 119; GPS shows it less than a hundred yards off being true north. Without GPS technology, ascertaining accurate directions was circumstantial due to topography and it does not reflect Wills' accuracy with a compass. Burke and Wills had left Camp 119 after breakfast, then lost time of, by my estimate, perhaps about two hours when Billy got bogged.[ix] Therefore they likely travelled about ten hours for a ground distance of sixteen and a half miles to get from Camp 119 to Camp 120. This estimate is based on the tough conditions, i.e., 1.6 miles per hour walked to cover the distance.

A strange coincidence happened at the amphitheatre. I decided to record a series of GPS positions to define the area for an accurate sketch. Eighteen spots were randomly selected as I walked around the perimeter and recorded in the GPS memory. When I plotted them, four were exactly due north of Camp 119. Eight were to the west and four to the east. A portion of the western section is below the "beach" level so could not be considered a good campsite in a very wet season.

CHAPTER 13: THE LAST CAMP

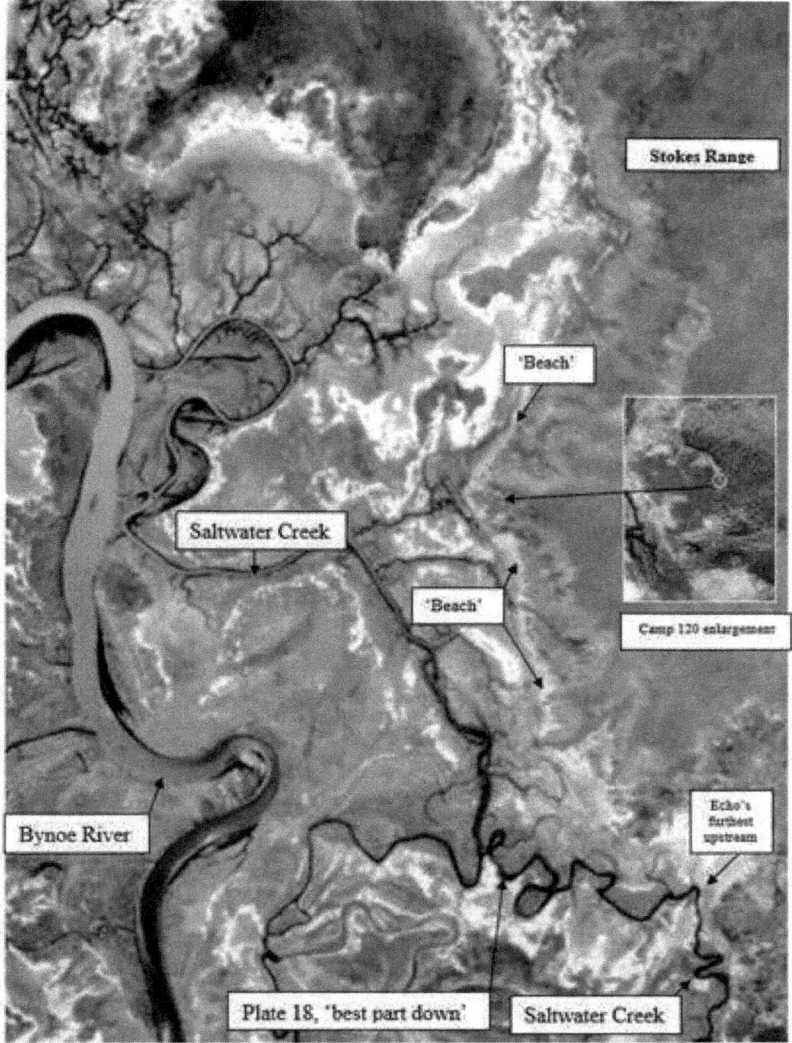

Choosing a site for Camp 120 with care was important to Burke and Wills. Less than one hundred yards of the site they chose would see them up on the cliff at an elevation of 20 metres as per the AUSLIG map. (See Camp 120 inset enlargement above.)

It is worth noting that Stokes' sketches were very similar.

This view was important for three reasons. It showed them that they were within two and a half miles of the river that they were following, and that that they were on the edge of the mangroves. Lastly, it gave them a good forward view of the best route to skirt the river the next day.

No glimpse of river water can be seen from this vantage point. Identifying the river requires spotting the line of higher mangroves. The whole 180° view of the western vista shows mangroves and mangrove fingers from the river.

The only blazed tree in the area of Camp 120 is this one Gutta-percha, which is a variety of mahogany, that has grown over. (See photo on the left.) This type of tree is a slow grower and is of small dimension — nine inches in diameter. It has been dated from a cross-section of a similar sized, dead Gutta-Percha from another non-historical area. I have discounted its connection with Burke and Wills due to its growth rate.

This tree is just starting to show some termite infestation in the centre of the blaze join. All gum varieties are suffering from white ant infestation, so the long-term survival chances of carved letters or numbers on gumtrees in this environment are minimal. Usually, Gutta-Percha trees are not affected by white ants. The area had been subject to a major fire many years ago.

Camp 120 would have been near the centre of the large amphitheatre — that is the only point that would meet their needs. With such ideal conditions, this was probably the point where the pair decided to leave Billy to rest and continue without him. Leichhardt's plan showed them to be less than five miles from their goal: the Gulf beach.

CHAPTER 14
DASH TO THE SEA

The answers to understanding their route and achievements over this section lie in the area's topography. The only written note about this section that researchers have found is the following one line: -

> Next morning we started at daybreak, leaving the horse short hobbled. [i]

This is the sole entry in Wills' diary for the 11th of February. No doubt they planned to walk as far and as fast northward as possible in a final effort to reach the sea.

Judging by the early hour of their departure, they were not delayed by rain and they were highly motivated to put in a long day. Leaving the horse, presumably with a lot of their equipment, was a serious decision as it left them defenceless and without transport or food — not forgetting that Billy was also on their future menu. [ii]

Two years later J.G. Macdonald lost one of his horses to local Aboriginal People for food just east of this area[iii] so the risk was a real one for Burke and Wills. The decision to leave the horse was probably taken because Billy was "completely baked" and the campsite offered the horse a concealed location with food, water and shade. Such a circumstance would have been virtually impossible to plan in advance and foolish to depend on existing along an unknown route.

Without any other written record of the day's travel, firsthand inspection on the ground provided an excellent opportunity to accurately determine where they travelled on that final day north. Apart from the obvious advantage of gaining access to remote areas, helicopters offered no help in working out Burke and Wills' route. There is no substitute for ground level inspection. Any number of experienced bush people given Burke and Wills' task today would come up with the same route north. Except for maybe a variation of a couple of hundred yards wide, they would all certainly finish on the same sandhill.

While flying over the area later we proved our theory, noting that the cattle had defined the same route but for a different reason. They travel the route each day to graze at the last sandhill and water near Camp 120. This single track is about two feet wide, which is ideal for people to walk along.

With a daybreak start, probably at 5am, they had up to fourteen hours of travel available to them at 1.6 miles per hour. This rate was based on their average over eleven "normal" days recorded in the previous month and totals to a day trip of 22 miles being well within their capabilities. First, they would have climbed the hill as mentioned before, and used their telescope and compass — that is, if they had not done so the previous evening, which they probably would have, given how excited and confident they would have been of seeing the sea.

They then would have decided on a dogleg course to clear the mangroves and put them on the next piece of high ground. The higher ground in this area offers very good walking conditions. They would not have continued north as that would have appeared to lead them away from the river. The general river direction would have been the shortest way to the sea, which Ludwig Leichhardt's map correctly notes. From Leichhardt's plan they would have incorrectly thought that the sea was just on the other side of the low northwest section of the Stokes Range.

Our excitement was palpable as we walked this section in the footsteps of Burke and Wills. To think that we were probably the only researchers apart from Frederick Walker, looking for them on horseback in 1862, to have traversed this important section since 1861 was enough to make our hearts beat faster. It was humbling to say the least, to think that these two men had walked most of the way from Melbourne to this very place at a time when the Gulf country was almost completely unknown. We take our hats off to you Mr Burke and Mr Wills.

Their first leg, 2 miles across the saline flats, would have been in a north-northwest direction skirting the intermediate mangroves to a point at about latitude 17° 38' 34", longitude 140° 48' 51". This would be the hardest section of the day as ground conditions here would have matched the previous day's route prior to the Saltwater Creek crossing, where Wills recorded "the ground we were taking was very boggy".[iv]

In 1846 John Lort Stokes described similar flats in the area as: -

> fringed with mangroves, behind which stretched extensive mud flats, which from being encrusted with salt and glistening in the sun were mistaken at first for sheets of water. [v]

This is an accurate description. See next page, a photo of the general area where Camp 120 is believed to have been located.

CHAPTER 14: DASH TO THE SEA

Overlooking the probable site of Camp 120 on the edge of the Stokes Range

Their next leg would have been in a northwest direction to a point of about latitude 17º 38' 07", longitude 140º 47' 49". They would probably have followed the "beach" for ease of walking. So far, they had travelled over 3.5 miles.

Following that they would have headed a little east of north to latitude 17º 37' 10", longitude 140º 48' until reaching a total of 4.66 miles travelled with good walking conditions.

Then their course would have been approximately north-northeast to a point latitude 17º 36' 25", longitude 140º 48' 28". Now having travelled 5.66 miles, they would be on the edge of the range at an elevation of about five feet above the plain. Leichhardt's "beach" sighting was east-northeast two miles by latitude and longitude; they could have had the same view from that point had it not been blocked by mangroves.

They were clear of the close mangroves to their left, many now dead and not shown on photos or maps, with a new vista appearing. The mangrove system of the Bynoe River could be seen in the distance to the northwest. They thought it was the Flinders River, having not noticed the point where it divided into two. A low ridge lay roughly three miles through a ten degree gap and then further east was a new mangrove system. This stretched to the east for the balance of their vista. From their perspective this could have been a new eastern river system, possibly the creeks shown by Arrowsmith on Leichhardt's plan that run into the stub of the Bynoe River.

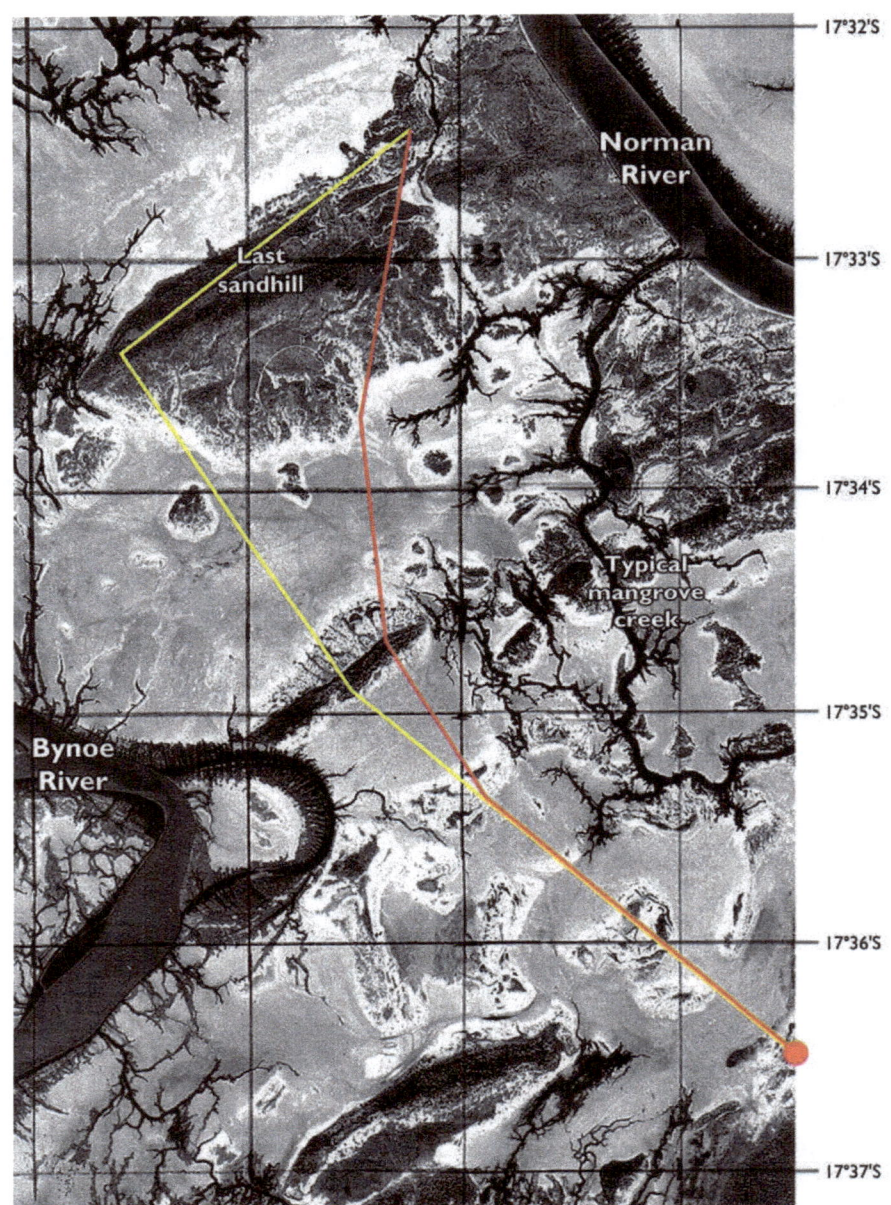

Sand flats north of Stokes Range Yellow track out to last sandhill, red return

They would have no alternative at this point but to head northwest to the low sand ridge over generally saline coastal flats below the level of the "beach". The sand ridges are ancient and well grassed with mature but scattered light timber. The ridge was reached after about two and a half miles; in total they had travelled 8.75 miles to latitude 17º 40' longitude 140º 46' 40".

The next ridge was in the same direction, i.e., northwest. This sand ridge is the most extensive in that area and runs from the Bynoe River to the Norman River trisected by two small creeks. The central section of this ridge lay 10.66 miles from camp at about latitude 17º 33' 24", longitude 140º 45' 24". They likely planned to shorten the return journey by a mile across the western section of the Stokes Range. This allowed them to use up a little over twenty of the twenty-two miles available to them in terms of time.

The terrain they walked was half saline flats and half grass covered sandy soil. Mangroves grew across their western vista and stretched to the north-northeast. Some of these were dead prior to 1966 and are not shown on AUSLIG maps or air photos from that time.

They were two miles southeast from where Mr Fitzmaurice of Stokes' party had turned back during his boat trip along the Bynoe River. From Leichhardt's map they would have thought they were west of that point.

Nearing the Gulf of Carpentaria

Their only practical option was following the ridge northeast for about one mile in hope of glimpsing the sea. From inspecting maps, we know that this is parallel with the coast. They probably suspected as such because sand hills near the sea are generally parallel to the coast. At this stage, allowing for two shortcuts, the total for the return journey would have been calculated at 21.25 miles.

This sand ridge is the final hurdle before the sea and lies, in reality, only 3.5 miles from the coast. However, both Stokes' Chart and Leichhardt's map showed it much further south. Leichhardt's map was the most recent for Wills and he would have relied more heavily on that than any other information.

Bear in mind that they thought they were on the Flinders River, not the Bynoe River. The Flinders is actually a tributary of the Bynoe as the Bynoe is the larger of the two rivers. Strictly speaking the names should be swapped. (See composite map on the next page.)

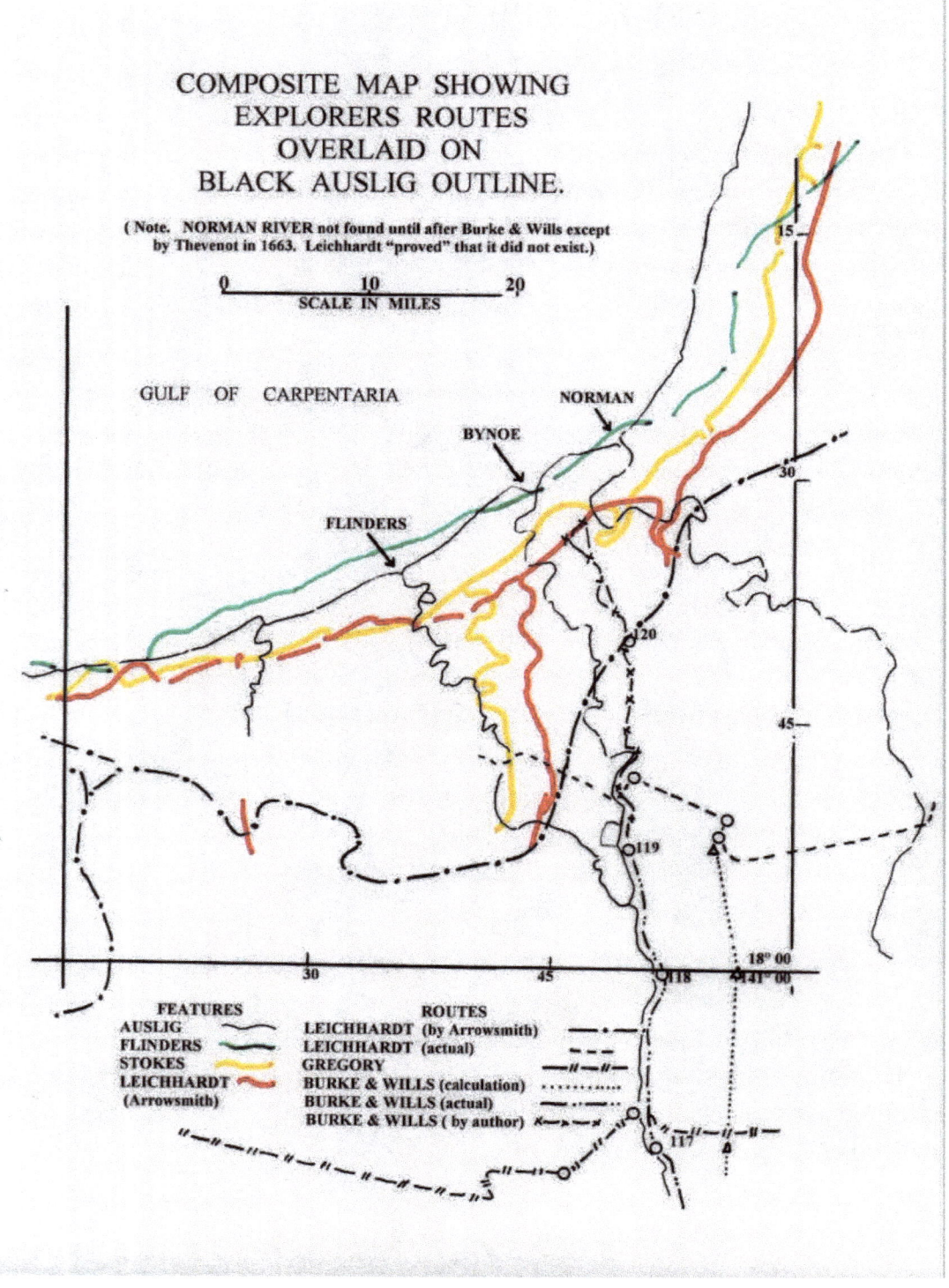

CHAPTER 14: DASH TO THE SEA

The view from the top of the sand ridge to the Gulf of Carpentaria was blocked only by the height of the mangroves. I tried to walk the length of this ridge along its highest part to inspect all the trees for blazes. Unfortunately, the top of the ridge is now infested with introduced rubber vines, which became a prevalent pest in the Gulf area early in the twentieth century. These vines were not there in Burke and Wills' time. Instead, I flew in a helicopter just south of the ridge to determine the height necessary to see the sea. Judging from the height of the existing trees we estimated Burke and Wills would have seen the sea if the sand ridge were just another forty feet higher. In the helicopter, we reached that extra forty feet altitude and saw across a line of mangroves to the mouth of the Bynoe River, which is the first place where the sea vista opens up.

I do not believe that they would have walked further onto the flats. From here on the travel would have been over 100% coastal saline flats that would have been very boggy. Stock tracks I saw indicated that cattle sink about nine inches into this ground in the aftermath of the Wet. People would sink in less than half that, and conditions would deteriorate as they approached the sea. They could not risk such difficult terrain on such a tight schedule. Remember, they had left much of their equipment and food at Camp 120.

They would have been devastated not to reach the beach or even see the sea. The only clue left was the river heading southwest where they abandoned it to head due north. Their estimation of distance would have hinted that Leichhardt's plan was flawed and that they had been misled by it.

Perhaps somewhere on this ridge was the spot where Burke formulated in his mind the sentence in his report stating: -

> It would be well to say we reached the sea, but we could not obtain a view of the open ocean, although we made every endeavour to do so. [vi]

He had written this comment on the 28th of March, meaning he waited over six weeks to record it.[vii] That delay might well be a measure of their disappointment.

Perhaps there is, or was, a blazed tree in the centre of this inaccessible, isolated sand ridge that is seldom visited by humans. Finding such evidence is the only way we could be more certain of knowing how far north they reached. The rubber vines prevent any inspection though there are not a great number of trees involved. For now, this on-site research demonstrates the highest degree of accuracy we have to conclude the mystery of Burke and Wills. And, as it stands, the on-site evidence is compelling.

Vista northwards from Camp 120

David at the monument we erected near Camp 120

Marking Camp 120

I have erected a low plaque in the area of Camp 120 behind where there may have been a blazed tree site. The plaque site was chosen due to topographic considerations — it makes no claim to being the exact spot. The plaque measures eight by four and a half inches and is about fifteen inches above ground within a small group of rocks. It is made of stainless steel, set in concrete, and the machine engraved plate is made of surgical grade stainless steel.

The plaque's "S.E." should read "S." We prepared it at home in Adelaide before we left to head north and could not update it on site.

Plaque at the monument erected near the site of Camp 120

Its GPS position is latitude 17° 39' 56", longitude 140° 49' 36". This is less than 4" off due north from the tree at Camp 119, a coincidence, but a remarkable one at that.

Camp 120 is a lonely, isolated site. It reflects the courage of Burke and Wills and will only ever be visited by very few people. No doubt Wills would have been very depressed, thinking that he had made a major error, but where? All his recent campsite positions had checked each other. Were his watches a long way out? If so, which river were they on, given watch errors only affected longitude? His notes would have offered no hint. They could not. He did not make a mistake, but he was never to know that. Only now, over a century later, can we confirm that he ranks with Australia's greatest early navigators.

History has deprived them of the achievement that they so valiantly strove towards and lost their lives for with a bittersweet irony. This irony is that the "beach" on the last sand hill's northern side is now littered with flotsam and jetsam, i.e., it is the actual beach during some of the annual king tide/storm cycles.

The present-day location features a large steel marine marker buoy with a long length of anchor chain that has been there many years (though its arrival must have been since mid-1966 as it is not evident on AUSLIG air photos from that time). We also found, among other things, a glass net covered fishing float with the net in a rotting state, green Asian plastic fishing buoys, 150 millimetres in length, orange plastic fishing crates and bottles.

Matthew Flinders found such materials nearby in the Sir Edward Pellew Group about sixty years before: -

> Besides pieces of earthen jars and trees cut with axes, we found remnants of bamboo lattice work, palm leaves sewed with cotton thread into the form of such hats as are warn [sic] by the Chinese, and the remains of blue cotton trousers, of the fashion called moormans. A wooden anchor of one flute, and three boats' rudders of violet wood were also found. [viii]

If they had found similar artefacts, would they have returned with a spring in their step back to Coopers Creek in time to change the tragic outcome of the Expedition?

CHAPTER 15
LAST WORDS

Wills observed and recorded objectively and accurately, without embellishment, to the end.

I imagine many people in his terminal situation would not continue contributing to the Expedition and to humanity's knowledge. But William Wills continued writing in his diary. At the time of writing, researchers are only now examining Will's "bush tucker" notes. We now know his observations about poison in the husk of the nardoo and its resulting symptoms are true.

In his diary he said: -

> Starvation on nardoo is by no means very unpleasant, but for the weakness one feels, and the utter inability to move one's self; for as far as appetite is concerned, it gives the greatest satisfaction. Certainly fat and sugar would be more to one's taste; in fact those seem to me to be the great stand-by for one in this extraordinary continent: not that I mean to depreciate the farinaceous food; but the want of sugar and fat in all substances obtainable here is so great that they become almost valueless to us as articles of food, without the addition of something else. (signed) W.J. Wills. [i]

Wills' attention to detail cannot be better understood than by reading the last entry in his diary, believed to be written on the day he died: -

> Friday, 29th June 1861. Clear cold night, slight breeze from the east, day beautifully warm and pleasant. Mr. Burke suffers greatly from the cold and is getting extremely weak; he and King start tomorrow up the creek to look for the blacks; it is our only chance we have of being saved from starvation. I am weaker than ever, although I have a good appetite and relish the nardoo much; but it seems to give us no nutriment, and the birds here are so shy as not to be got at. Even if we got a good supply of fish, I doubt whether we could do much work on them and the nardoo alone. Nothing now but the greatest good luck can save any of us; and as for myself I may live four or five days if the weather continues warm. My pulse is forty-eight, and very weak, and my legs and arms are nearly skin and bone. I can only look out, like Mr Micawber, "for something to turn up".

CHAPTER 15: LAST WORDS

Mystery solved. We now know exactly where Burke and Wills were for those last three days north of Camp 119. Together with only the horse Billy and carrying minimal rations, the pair pushed on in the belief that they could reach the sea.

But was the fatal Expedition a failure, as decades of researchers thought? While they did not see the sea, to all intents and purposes they reached the coastline — at least as it was during king tides. Wills' navigation can only be called exceptional, given that he used relatively primitive instruments and had maps and charts containing serious errors and omissions.

To have navigated the Expedition nearly three thousand kilometres from Melbourne to the Gulf of Carpentaria and back to Cooper's Creek was an incredible feat. To do so over almost completely unknown territory and in some of the most inhospitable land in the world in 1860/61 speaks highly of Wills' competence and was little short of miraculous.

William John Wills, we salute you.

> Lives of great men all remind us
> We can make our lives sublime,
> And departing leave behind us
> Footsteps on the sands of time;
> Footprints that perhaps another,
> Sailing o'er Life's solemn main,
> A forlorn and shipwreck'd brother,
> Seeing, shall take heart again.
>
> —William Wadsworth Longfellow

APPENDIX 1

4WD Bike Set Up for the Bush

Our needs were very specific, and the following items were added: -

We named the bike GOLAH, after Burke and Wills' camel that was abandoned in the Gulf area and whose tracks Walker saw in his search for Burke and Wills. The name was inscribed / painted / written above the headlight and on each side of the headlight was the word "Surveyor". This was for property owners' benefit when we made a minor quick excursion on an adjoining property without permission.

The tubeless tyres were treated by an internal self-sealing "slime" inserted via the valve. Plugs were carried for large holes as well as an additional can of slime.

The front rack had factory rails fitted to contain equipment. We added a pair of quick-release rifle mounts to the back of the rack so we could access the rifle without leaving the driving position — a necessary specification when working in crocodile and feral pig territory. The front of the quad had a WARN electric winch and its switch sat just next to the rider's left knee. To increase the retrieval capacity of the winch, we added a webbing strap and shackle to go around a tree and hold a ball bearing snatch block. This doubled the pulling power of the winch. You can source commercial ones for 4WD vehicles but without ball bearings and they carry too great a weight handicap for a quad, so I designed and built one myself. However, I could only make the pulley in brass due to the limitations of my lathe. A friend made one for me in stainless steel using my brass one as a model. The result was a very satisfactory and light piece of safety equipment.

Below the winch, we covered the radiator with the extra protection of a wire grill and double thickness bird wire to intercept grass seeds as we typically travelled through grass 50–100 centimetres high. The bull bar carried a security chain to secure and lock the quad to the vehicle, tree, post etc. as they are a favourite target of thieves. We have even been stopped by the South Australian police highway patrol to ensure that we were not carrying a stolen 4WD bike.

We designed special cargo bags to attach to the front and rear cargo racks. These were made from red plastic covered canvas typically used in semi-trailer goods covers. The front one was 16 centimetres wide and the rear was 20 centimetres, both fastened by zippers on their rear top edge. Between the back of the front one and the rifle was a canvas map bag with all the day's search information. Under the front skid plate, a stainless-steel threaded ring allowed us a quick and efficient tie-down of the front of the quad on the Toyota with a marine snap shackle.

The handlebars had an added aluminium frame to carry two GPS devices and a compass, which had been swung and adjusted so the readings remained accurate even near metal. To keep the GPS powered, we had a cable to charge it from the 4WD bike's power. (We also carried spare GPS batteries).

An electric tyre pump was stored in the under-seat toolbox. The battery had been upgraded from a wet to dry to overcome the loss of battery fluid, as it tended to spill during transit.

The rear of the rear rack had a frame with about eighty metres of plasma line. This material can extend the range of the winch should a suitable tree be further away. The rear bag held a sand anchor and folding shovel should we be on sand. The bags carried four folding sand/mud mats, a hand chainsaw, a first aid kit, a satellite emergency beacon, signal mirror, food and water. Our tree-marking gear included aluminium plates, metal letter punches, hammer, steel plate, battery-electric drill, drills, monel metal nails, side cutters, chisel plus photographic gear.

We wore gloves with fingertips exposed to enable handling photos, pencils, rifle, GPS etc. Wraparound sunglasses are good for protection from insects and the sun. Earplugs on strings were attached to each of our lapels for quick use in case the rifle must be used. We were both confident in each other's ability with the firearm. Because the rifle must be used at extremely short notice, we could not wear motorbike helmets though we did have them.

The rear of the 4WD bike was fitted with a light tow ball that matched a light trailer hitch. This allowed us to quickly fit the tie down of the bike's rear on the Toyota using a small lever and chain tie down.

We also carried a first aid kit and a satellite phone as well as a two-way radio which was of little use in the bush given its limited range.

APPENDIX 2

The following, written by David Hillan, was the basis of the 1999 application to list the site of Camp 119 as a significant heritage location and to have the Carpentaria Shire Council upgrade the Camp 119 site.

BURKE & WILLS' CAMP CXIX

Welcome to a special place in the history of exploration in Australia. It meets the following criteria:

(a) the place is important in demonstrating the evolution and pattern of Australia's and Queensland's history

(b) the place demonstrates rare, uncommon, or endangered aspects of Australia's and Queensland's cultural heritage

(c) the place has the potential to yield information that will contribute to an understanding of Queensland's and Australia's history

(d) the place is important in demonstrating the principal characteristics of a particular class of places

(e) the place is important in demonstrating a high degree of creative or technical achievement at a particular period

(f) the place has a special association with the life work of a particular person, group or organization of importance in Australia's and Queensland's history

These six criteria are collectively covered as follows.

Burke and Wills' Camp **B/CXIX** is 35 kilometres southwest of Normanton, about two kilometres south of the Normanton to Burketown road and about 200 metres to the east of the Little Bynoe River. Its location is latitude 17°52.718S, longitude 140°49.585E, datum WGS84. It is located within MAGOWRA station.

This is arguably the most asset rich of the entire Burke and Wills' campsites across Australia for the reasons set out below. Whilst I live on the opposite side of Australia, I have spent a lot of time over many years researching the Burke and Wills'

Expedition in the northern area and have been to this site many times over the last eleven years. The general area has produced a lot of unpublished information. My interest has not been focused only on this site so my discoveries on it are incidental to my research. The full story of these National Assets seem to be periodically lost to Australians so now they should be officially recognized and identified, with suitable signage, to prevent them being forgotten again and even inadvertently destroyed, which as you will see, is a very real possibility. Indeed, one blazed tree has been destroyed by Council grading activities since 1999.

Burke and Wills left Gray and King at this camp for three days whilst they, and their horse Billy, pushed north towards the sea. Fifteen trees were blazed to mark the site though possibly only two were marked by Wills and the others by the two men left in the camp for three days.

Walker, in his search for Burke and Wills eleven months later, found these blazed trees. He recorded that one was marked **B** over **CXIX**, and one was marked **S.SE 14**. He dug 14 inches, 14 feet and 14 yards and found nothing on the compass course South, South East, noting in his personal diary of the 8/1/1862 "that the ground had never been opened up and would require a pickaxe to make much way into it.'

Walker marked a tree FW/12 Jan/1862 and that tree is the feature of the site now and is the sole focus of tourist attention. It is generally thought to be the Burke and Wills tree. He noted that this camp was about three quarters of a mile from his camp where they had been based for about four days.

The staff at Magowra station found Walker's tree and other blazed trees at the site in 1909 and advised the Queensland Geographical Society. They sent their Secretary to the area to inspect the discovery and confirm it as Burke and Wills' Camp 119. Thomson arrived at the site and noticed another tree that had been overlooked by the staff and that was the **B/CXIX** tree. The **B** was still faintly visible but the **CXIX** had eroded out in the 48 years since.

Thomson carried out a compass and tape survey of the site and photographed all or most of the trees. His report, plan and photographs were published in the Queensland Geographical Journal, 25th Session, 1909-1910, Vol xxv. The survey plan is greatly reduced and at that scale is useless as a guide. I have re-established it by laser enlargement to the original scale to aid tree identification. My attention was drawn to the existence of this information by Queensland Surveyor, Richard Cork, in 1998.

APPENDIX

Stumps of Gutta Percha, numbers 1 and 6, dead Gutta Percha numbers 2 and 3 Stump 1 gone by October 1999; photo taken mid-1999

During his visit the previous year he identified some trees, but he did not have a tape, so I took one with me into the area and carried out a detailed survey. This has produced surprising results. Contrary to local belief most of the trees still exist, see survey table which follows [Appendix 3] and photo above.

Plan of trees at Camp 119

Tree 6 at Normanton Railway Museum

Tree 6 was sawn off several years ago and whilst the sawn stump is still in existence, the blazed section of the tree is in the Normanton Railway museum. Artefacts were found by the staff of Magowra Station in later years buried in a Camp Oven.

A camp oven like the one buried at Camp 119

These included a Mercury Artificial Horizon used by Wills for his astronomical observations. I believe that the only way the staff could have found this equipment was for it to have been accidentally exposed. This would only have been possible by the bank of the lagoon having been slowly eroded out by cattle drinking at the water's edge. Walker's failure to find the oven was because he did not realise that Surveyors used Links as a unit of measurement and not yards, feet or inches. 14 links equals 9' 3". We can deduce with a high degree of certainty that the tree was Thomson's no 13.

A more important factor emerges for Burke and Wills' researchers and that is the **B/CXIX** tree (number 12 by Thomson), proven both by survey and photo from 1909/10 to be authentic, allows measurements to be taken of the shield (height above ground, height of blaze, width of blaze, then and now), i.e. its "signature", that will assist in identifying other genuine B&W blazed trees at least north of Coopers Creek. In a survey party the blazing was usually carried out by the same person, hence a "signature". One tree north of Coopers Creek has already been identified by others using this "signature". I believe that I have identified three others at Camps 101, 117 and 118.

All the blazes at 119 of Burke and Wills could be described as timid; they do not demand attention, the very purpose of a blaze. (Walker's does not meet this criticism). Indeed, I inspected tree 10 closely several times and could not find a blaze.

APPENDIX

After it was positively identified as an original by survey, I found two blazes close to the ground that were definitely made with an axe. A close inspection of Thomson's photos suggests that there was a depression running across the site generally following the Gutta-perchas, hence the ground filling up to and perhaps over some of the blazes. Frank Clune's 1936 photo on page 125 of *Dig: A Drama of Central Australia* might confirm this.

In 1998 the **B** tree was heavily infested with rubber vine and its bulk was threatening the survival of the **B** tree due to weight, smothering and flood loading. We spent two days trying to remove the vines but only succeeded on the lower three metres. The aid of the Lions Club of Carpentaria was enlisted. With the aid of three members and an eight-metre ladder the tree was granted the opportunity of a new lease of life.

In 1998 I also located a tree at Walker's camp 545 metres away, "as the crow flies", it was from this camp that Walker's men found Camp 119. Its position is lat. 17° 52' 26" long. 140° 49' 42" (WGS84).

Walker's notes and logic placed me six paces from the blaze. (My hair stood on end). It is believed that this is the first documented identification since 1862. Its presence should be included with Camp 119 in your visit and for the understanding of this site.

Tourists and researchers to the Camp 119 site only see Walker's tree so should use this information to fully view the site. Minimal signage had faded by 2002 and was unreadable.

APPENDIX 3

Burke and Wills' marked trees at Camp 119

Bearings and distances measured from Walker's tree marked: -

FW
12 Jan
1862

	By Thomson		By David Hillan		
Number	Bearing	Distance	Bearing	Distance	Comments
1	172° 30'	26'11"	171° 30'	26'11"	Stump
2	178° 30'	47' 7"	176° 30'	47' 9"	Dead gutta-percha
3	177° 00'	52'10"	176° 00	53'9 ½"	Dead gutta-percha
4	170° 00'	59' 0 ½"			
5	168° 00'	60' 8"	168° 00'	57' 1"	Stump?
6	167° 00'	62' 8"	165° 00'	64'7 ½"	Stump/sawn
7	155° 00'	67' 3"			
8	166° 30'	129' 7"	163° 00'	129'11"	Dead gutta-percha
9	173° 30'	219'10"			
10	269° 00'	63'11½"	265° 30'	64'11½"	Dead gutta-percha
11	25° 00'	9'10"			
12	274° 30'	122' 5"	270° 30'	121'8 ½"	**B CXIX**
13	244° 00'	121' 4½"	244° 00'	123'0 ½"	Live coolabah
14	214° 30'	85' 3½"	213° 00'	85'3 ½"	Live coolabah
15	172° 00'	118' 1½"			
Monument	NA	NA	60° 00'	15'2"	Concrete

Distances in feet.
(1 foot = 0.3048 meters = 1.51 links)

Original dimensions scaled from J. P. Thomson's survey of the site and published "Expedition to The Gulf of Carpentaria, 1909-10" in *Queensland Geographical Journal*, 25th Session. Plan enlarged by laser print to original scale.

Field measurements by David Hillan with marine compass read to and from. Survey tape measurement along ground to eliminate sag.

Thomson's procedure not known.

There should be a minor compass bearing error as a result of change in magnetic poles over the 140 years. The variation detected is consistent in direction.

Variation on 12 is mainly due to tree leaning further north than in 1909.

Monument connection is as a survey reference mark for re-establishment of sites if Walker's tree is destroyed.

REFERENCES

Astronomical Observations. Box 2083/1/c, Australian Manuscript Collection, State Library of Victoria.

Beckler, Hermann. *A Journey to Coopers Creek.* Translated by Stephen Jeffries and Michael Kertesz. Melbourne: Melbourne University Press at the Miegunyah Press in association with the State Library of Victoria, 1993.

Bonyhady, Tim. *Burke and Wills: From Melbourne to Myth.* Sydney: David Ell Press, 1991.

The Burke and Wills exploring expedition: an account of the crossing of the continent of Australia, from Cooper's Creek to Carpentaria, with biographical sketches of Robert O'Hara Burke and William John Wills. Melbourne: Wilson and Mackinnon, 1861. Facsimile edition. Adelaide: Libraries Board of South Australia, 1963.

Cathcart, Michael. *Manning Clark's History of Australia.* Abridged. Melbourne: Melbourne University Press, 1993.

Clark, C.M.H. *A History of Australia.* Vol. 3. Melbourne: Melbourne University Press, 1978.

Clark, David. *Plane and Geodetic Surveying.* 2 vols. 1923. Reprint, London: Constable, 1923.

Clune, Frank. *Dig: The Burke and Wills Saga.* Sydney: Angus and Robertson, 1947.

Ellery, R.L.J. *Astronomical observations made at the Williamstown Observatory, 1861, 62 and 63.* Melbourne: John Ferres, Government Printer, 1869.

Ember, Steve and Bob Doughty. "The Story of Finding Longitude: It Was All a Question of Timing." *VOA Special English: EXPLORATIONS.* Voice of America. April 1, 2008. https://learningenglish.voanews.com/a/a-23-2008-04-01-voa1-83136127/128333.html

Favenc, Ernest. *The History of Australian Exploration 1788–1888.* Sydney: Turner and Henderson, 1888. Facsimile edition. Sydney: Golden Press, 1983.

Fenner, Charles. "Two Historic Gumtrees", reprinted from *Proceedings of the Royal Geographical Society, South Australian Branch, Session 1927–8*. Adelaide: Register Newspapers, 1928?.

Flinders, Mathew. *A Voyage to Terra Australis.* 2 vols. London: G&W Nicol, 1814. Facsimile edition. Adelaide: Libraries Board of South Australia, 1966.

Gregory, Augustus Charles and Francis Thomas. *Journals of Australian Explorations.* Brisbane: Gov. printer, 1884. Facsimile edition. Adelaide: Libraries Board of South Australia, 1969.

Gregory, Augustus Charles. Letter book, 1862. Survey Department, Brisbane.

Hiddins, Les. *Bush Tucker Man: Stories of Exploration and Survival.* Sydney: ABC Books, 1996.

Jackson, Andrew. *Robert O'Hara Burke and the Australian Exploration Expedition of 1860.* London: Smith, Elder, 1862.

Kerr, Collin and Margaret Kerr. *Australian Explorers.* Adelaide: Rigby, 1978.

Landsborough, William. *Journal Of Landsborough's Expedition from Carpentaria, In Search of Burke and Wills.* Melbourne: Bailliere, 1862. Facsimile edition. Adelaide: Libraries Board of South Australia, 1963.

Leichhardt, Dr Ludwig. *Dr. Ludwig Leichhardt's Letters from Australia: During years March 23, 1842, to April 3, 1848.* Translated and edited by L. L. Politzer. Melbourne: Pan Publishers, 1944.

Leichhardt, Dr Ludwig. *Journal of an Overland Expedition in Australia: From Moreton Bay to Port Essington 1844–1845.* London: T&W Boone, 1847. Facsimile edition. Adelaide: Libraries Board of South Australia, 1964.

Logan Jack, Robert. *Northmost Australia, three centuries of exploration, discovery, and adventure in and around the Cape York peninsular.* Vol. 1. London: Simpkin, Marshall, Hamilton, Kent, 1921.

Macdonald, J. G. *Journal of J.G. Macdonald on an expedition to the Gulf of Carpentaria and back.* Melbourne: George Slater, 1865. Facsimile edition. Brisbane: Corkwood Press, 1994.

McKinlay, John. *McKinlay's Journal of Exploration in the Interior of Australia: Burke Relief Expedition.* Melbourne: Bailliere, 1862. Facsimile edition. Adelaide: The Libraries Board of South Australia, 1962.

Perrin, Les. *The Mystery of the Leichhardt Survivor.* Stafford: L. Perrin, 1991.

Rocketfrog. *Burke and Wills Track.* August 12, 2006. *Wikimedia Commons.* https://commons.wikimedia.org/w/index.php?curid=4173494.

Sargent, Clem. "The royal Australian survey corps, 1915 – 1990." *Australian Surveyor* 39, no. 4 (December 1994): 275–289.

Scurfield, G. in collaboration with J.M. Scurfield. *The Hoddle Years: Surveying in Victoria, 1836–1853.* Canberra: The Institution of Surveyors, Paragon Printers, 1995.

Slater, Peter, Pat Slater, and Raoul Slater. *The Slater Field Guide to Australian Birds.* Sydney: Weldon Publishing, 1992.

Smith, Dick. *Australian GPS Location Guide.* Terrey Hills: Dick Smith Adventure, 1996.

Sobel, Dava. *Longitude.* London: Fourth Estate, 1996.

Stokes, J. Lort. *Discoveries in Australia.* Vol. 2. London: T&W Boone, 1846. Facsimile edition. Adelaide: Libraries Board of South Australia, 1969.

Sweetapple, Pam. "Les Henry," Obituaries, Daily Sun, April 14, 1987.

Thomson, J. P. *Expedition to the Gulf of Carpentaria.* Vol. 25, Queensland Geographical Journal, 1909-1910. Queensland: Royal Geographical society of Australia, 1910.

Walker, Frederick. Personal Diary. Box 2088A/3c (3), Australian Manuscripts Collection, State Library of Victoria, Melbourne.

Wills, Dr William John and William Wills. *A Successful Exploration Through The Interior of Australia, from Melbourne to the Gulf of Carpentaria.* London: Richard Bentley, 1863. Facsimile edition. Adelaide: The Friends of the State Library of South Australia, 1996.

NOTES

Wills, Dr William John. Astronomical observations, 31st August to 4th October 1860. Box 2083/1©, Victorian Exploring Expedition, Latrobe Library, Melbourne.

Wills, Dr William John. Astronomical observations, Swan Hill, 7th Sept 1860. Box 2084/6(a-f), Victorian Exploring Expedition, Latrobe Library, Melbourne.

NOTES

Introduction

i Rocketfrog, *Burke and Wills Track*, August 12, 2006, *Wikimedia Commons*, https://commons.wikimedia.org/w/index.php?curid=4173494.

Chapter 1

i Mathew Flinders, *A Voyage to Terra Australis* (London: G&W Nicol, 1814; Adelaide, Libraries Board of South Australia, 1966), 2:229.

ii Flinders, *Voyage to Terra Australis*, 2:230.

iii Flinders, *Voyage to Terra Australis*, 2:232–33.

Chapter 3

i Robert Logan Jack, *Northmost Australia, three centuries of exploration, discovery, and adventure in and around the Cape York peninsular*, vol. 1. (London: Simpkin, Marshall, Hamilton, Kent, 1921), 274.

ii Clem Sargent, *Centre fold map* in "The royal Australian survey corps, 1915 – 1990," Australian Surveyor 39, no. 4 (December 1994), 275–289.

iii Clem Sargent, "The royal Australian survey corps, 1915 – 1990," Australian Surveyor 39, no. 4 (December 1994), 281.

Chapter 5

i J. Lort Stokes, *Discoveries in Australia* (London: T&W Boone, 1846; Adelaide: Libraries Board of South Australia, 1969), 2:294.

Chapter 6

i Dr William John Wills and William Wills, *A Successful Exploration Through The Interior of Australia, from Melbourne to the Gulf of Carpentaria* (London: Richard Bentley, 1863; Adelaide: The Friends of the State Library of South Australia, 1996), 194, 197, 201.

ii Wills and Wills, *Successful Exploration*, 208.

iii Tim Bonyhady, *Burke and Wills: From Melbourne to Myth* (Sydney: David Ell Press, 1991), 128.

iv Wills and Wills, *Successful Exploration*, 204.

v Wills and Wills, *Successful Exploration*, 205.

vi John McKinlay, *McKinlay's Journal of Exploration in the Interior of Australia: Burke Relief Expedition* (Melbourne: Bailliere, 1862; Adelaide: The Libraries Board of South Australia, 1962), 88.

vii *The Burke and Wills exploring expedition: an account of the crossing of the continent of Australia, from Cooper's Creek to Carpentaria, with biographical sketches of Robert O'Hara Burke and William John Wills* (Melbourne: Wilson and Mackinnon, 1861; Adelaide: Libraries Board of South Australia, 1963), 33.

viii Andrew Jackson, *Robert O'Hara Burke and the Australian Exploration Expedition of 1860* (London: Smith, Elder, 1862), 222.

ix Wills and Wills, *Successful Exploration*, 223.

Chapter 7

i David Clark, *Plane and Geodetic Surveying*, rev. ed. (1923; repr., London: Constable, 1923), 2:73.

ii William John Wills, astronomical observations 31st August to 4th October 1860, Box 2083/1©, Victorian Exploring Expedition, Latrobe Library, Melbourne: 32–33.

iii Frank Clune, *Dig: A Drama of Central Australia* (Sydney: Angus and Robertson, 1947), 269.

iv Flinders, *Voyage to Terra Australis*, 1:16.

v Dr Ludwig Leichhardt, *Journal of an Overland Expedition in Australia: From Moreton Bay to Port Essington 1844–1845* (London: T&W Boone, 1847; Adelaide: Libraries Board of South Australia, 1964), 14.

vi Dava Sobel, *Longitude* (London: Fourth Estate, 1996), 117.

vii Stokes, *Discoveries in Australia*, 1:398.

viii Stokes, *Discoveries in Australia*, 1:51.

ix Clark, *Plane and Geodetic Surveying*, rev. ed., 2:74.

x Flinders, *Voyage to Terra Australis*, 1:24

xi Clark, *Plane and Geodetic Surveying*, rev. ed., 2:74.

xii Flinders, *Voyage to Terra Australis*, 2:161–62.

xiii Flinders, *Voyage to Terra Australis*, 2:216.

xiv Dr William John Wills, astronomical observations, Swan Hill, 7th Sept 1860, Box 2084/6(a-f), Victorian Exploring Expedition, Latrobe Library, Melbourne.

xv Dr William John Wills, astronomical observations 31st August to 4th October 1860, 33.

xvi R.L.J. Ellery, *Astronomical observations made at the Williamstown Observatory, 1861, 62 and 63* (Melbourne: John Ferres, Government Printer, 1869), 1–2.

xvii Dick Smith, *Australian GPS Location Guide* (Terrey Hills: Dick Smith Adventure, 1996), 20.

xviii Augustus Charles Gregory, letter book, 1862, Survey Department, Brisbane, 94.

xix Ernest Favenc, *The History of Australian Exploration 1788–1888* (Sydney: Turner and Henderson, 1888; Sydney: Golden Press, 1983), 213.

xx Flinders, *Voyage to Terra Australis*, 2:502–3.

Chapter 8

i Matthew Flinders, cartographer, *North Coast*, in *A Voyage to Terra Australis* (London: G&W Nicol, 1814; Adelaide: Libraries Board of South Australia, 1966), sheet 2.

ii Augustus Charles Gregory and Francis Thomas, *Journals of Australian Explorations* (Brisbane: Gov. printer, 1884; Adelaide: Libraries Board of South Australia, 1969), 174.

iii Gregory and Thomas, *Journals of Australian Explorations*, 175.

iv Dr Ludwig Leichhardt, April 18, 1846, in *Dr. Ludwig Leichhardt's Letters from Australia: During years March 23, 1842, to April 3, 1848*, trans. and ed. L. L. Politzer (Melbourne: Pan Publishers,1944), 54.

v Logan Jack, *Northmost Australia*, 1:196.

vi Wills and Wills, *Successful Exploration*, 33.

vii G. Scurfield and J.M. Scurfield, *The Hoddle Years: Surveying in Victoria, 1836–1853* (Canberra: The Institution of Surveyors, Paragon Printers, 1995), 42.

viii Scurfield and Scurfield, *The Hoddle Years*, 44.

ix Stokes, *Discoveries in Australia*, 1:307.

x Stokes, *Discoveries in Australia*, 2:367.

xi Stokes, *Discoveries in Australia*, 1:16.

xii Wills and Wills, *Successful Exploration*, 153.

xiii William Landsborough, *Journal Of Landsborough's Expedition From Carpentaria, In Search of Burke and Wills* (Melbourne: Bailliere, 1862; Adelaide: Libraries Board of South Australia, 1963), 70.

xiv Wills and Wills, *Successful Exploration*, 209–10.

xv Leichhardt, *Overland Expedition in Australia*, 337.

xvi Leichhardt, *Overland Expedition in Australia*, 333.

xvii Leichhardt, *Overland Expedition in Australia*, 14.

xviii Flinders, *Voyage to Terra Australis*, 2:132.

xix Stokes, *Discoveries in Australia*, 1:27.

xx Stokes, *Discoveries in Australia*, 2:324.

xxi Stokes, *Discoveries in Australia*, 2:324.

xxii Flinders, *Voyage to Terra Australis,* 1:8–9.

xxiii Stokes, *Discoveries in Australia,* 1:21.

xxiv Stokes, *Discoveries in Australia,* 2:303.

xxv Stokes, *Discoveries in Australia,* 2:324.

xxvi A. G. L. Shaw and C. M. H. Clark, *Australian Dictionary of Biography* (Melbourne: Melbourne University Press, 1979), 2:488.

xxvii Frederick Walker, Personal Diary, Dec 30, 1861, Box 2088A/3c (3), Australian Manuscripts Collection, State Library of Victoria, Melbourne.

xxviii McKinlay, *McKinlay's Journal of Exploration,* 88.

xxix McKinlay, *McKinlay's Journal of Exploration,* 99.

xxx McKinlay, *McKinlay's Journal of Exploration,* Sheet 2.

xxxi Hermann Beckler, Map in *A Journey to Cooper's Creek,* trans. Stephen Jeffries and Michael Kertesz. (Melbourne: Miegunyah Press with the State Library of Victoria, 1993).

Chapter 9

i Les Hiddins, *Bush Tucker Man: Stories of Exploration and Survival* (Sydney: ABC Books, 1996), 92.

ii Charles Fenner, "Two Historic Gumtrees", reprinted from *Proceedings of the Royal Geographical Society, South Australian Branch, Session 1927–8* (Adelaide: Register Newspapers, 1928?), 6.

iii J. P. Thomson, *Expedition to the Gulf of Carpentaria,* vol. 25, *Queensland Geographical Journal, 1909-1910* (Queensland: Royal Geographical society of Australia, 1910), 66.

iv J. G. Macdonald, *Journal of J.G. Macdonald on an expedition to the Gulf of Carpentaria and back* (Melbourne: George Slater, 1865), 15.

Chapter 10

i Wills and Wills, *Successful Exploration,* 213–214.

ii Wills and Wills, *Successful Exploration,* 210–13.

iii Stokes, *Discoveries in Australia,* 2:76.

iv McKinlay, *McKinlay's Journal of Exploration,* 99.

v Landsborough, *Landsborough's Expedition From Carpentaria,* 10.

vi Logan Jack, *Northmost Australia,* 1:4.

vii Wills and Wills, *Successful Exploration,* 194–95.

viii Wills and Wills, *Successful Exploration,* 211.

NOTES

Chapter 11

i Wills and Wills, *Successful Exploration*, 33–34.

ii Astronomical Observations, Box 2083/1/c, Australian Manuscript Collection, State Library of Victoria: 33.

iii Wills and Wills, *Successful Exploration*, 224.

iv Les Perrin, *The Mystery of the Leichhardt Survivor* (Stafford: L. Perrin, 1991), 35.

v Wills and Wills, *Successful Exploration*, 31–33.

vi *Burke and Wills Exploring Expedition* (Melbourne, 1861), 36.

vii Scurfield and Scurfield, *The Hoddle Years*, 20.

viii Wills and Wills, *Successful Exploration*, 50.

ix Wills and Wills, *Successful Exploration*, 52.

x Wills and Wills, *Successful Exploration*, 50.

xi Wills and Wills, *Successful Exploration*, 51–55.

xii Wills and Wills, *Successful Exploration*, 93.

xiii William John Wills, astronomical observations 31st August to 4th October 1860, 32–33, 173.

xiv Wills and Wills, *Successful Exploration*, 183.

xv Stokes, *Discoveries in Australia*, 2:88.

xvi Stokes, *Discoveries in Australia*, 2:413–14.

xvii Stokes, *Discoveries in Australia*, 2:108–9.

xviii Flinders, *Voyage to Terra Australis*, 2:54.

xix Flinders, *Voyage to Terra Australis*, 1:162, 256.

xx Stokes, *Discoveries in Australia*, 2:67.

xxi Leichhardt, *Overland Expedition in Australia*, 14.

xxii C.M.H Clark, *A History of Australia*, (Melbourne: Melbourne University Press, 1978), 3:151.

xxiii Michael Cathcart, *Manning Clark's History of Australia* (Melbourne: Melbourne University Press, 1993), 286.

xxiv Clark, *Plane and Geodetic Surveying*, rev. ed., 2:64.

xxv Stokes, *Discoveries in Australia*, 1:421.

xxvi Flinders, *Voyage to Terra Australis*, 1:256.

xxvii Wills and Wills, *Successful Exploration*, 217.

xxviii Peter Slater, Pat Slater, and Raoul Slater, *The Slater Field Guide to Australian Birds* (Sydney: Weldon Publishing, 1992), 184.

xxix Flinders, *Voyage to Terra Australis*, 2:145.

xxx Wills and Wills, *Successful Exploration*, 220.

xxxi Wills and Wills, *Successful Exploration*, 220.

xxxii Wills and Wills, *Successful Exploration*, 221.

xxxiii Clifford Frith and Dawn Frith, *Australian Tropical Reptiles and Frogs* (Malanda: Frith & Frith, 1991), 47.

Chapter 12

i Leichhardt, *Overland Expedition in Australia*, 333.

ii Woodburn, John. Normanton resident with historical interests.

iii Walker, Personal Diary, Dec 30, 1861.

iv Thomson, *Expedition to the Gulf of Carpentaria*, 65.

v Franke Clune, photo of blazed tree "FW 1862", November 1936, *Dig: A Drama of Central Australia* (Sydney: Angas and Robertson, 1947), 145, facing photo 252.

vi Woodburn, John. Normanton resident with historical interests.

vii Walker, Personal Diary, Dec 30, 1861.

viii Tom Bergin, *In the Steps of Burke and Wills* (Sydney: ABC, 1981).

ix Wills and Wills, *Successful Exploration*, 143.

x Wills and Wills, *Successful Exploration*, 149.

xi Beckler, *A Journey To Cooper's Creek*, 141.

xii Wills and Wills, *Successful Exploration*, 212.

xiii Beckler, *A Journey To Cooper's Creek*, 113.

xiv Beckler, *A Journey To Cooper's Creek*, 66–69.

xv Wills and Wills, *Successful Exploration*, 210.

xvi Wills and Wills, *Successful Exploration*, 211.

xvii Wills and Wills, *Successful Exploration*, 211.

xviii Wills and Wills, *Successful Exploration*, 213.

xix Collin Kerr and Margaret Kerr, *Australian Explorers* (Adelaide: Rigby, 1978), 55.

xx Stokes, *Discoveries in Australia,* 1:424.

xxi Wills and Wills, *Successful Exploration,* 210.

xxii Stokes, *Discoveries in Australia,* 2:36–37.

xxiii Woodburn, John. Normanton resident with historical interests.

xxiv Pam Sweetapple, "Les Henry," Obituaries, *Daily Sun,* April 14, 1987.

xxv Walker, Personal Diary, Jan 1, 1862.

xxvi Leichhardt, *Overland Expedition in Australia,* 341.

xxvii *Burke and Wills Exploring Expedition* (Melbourne, 1861), 33.

xxviii Wills and Wills, *Successful Exploration,* 213.

Chapter 13

i Wills and Wills, *Successful Exploration,* 213.

ii Walker, Personal Diary, Jan 1, 1862.

iii Wills and Wills, *Successful Exploration,* 212.

iv Walker, Personal Diary, Jan 2, 1862.

v Walker, Personal Diary, Jan 3, 1862.

vi Walker, Personal Diary, Jan 1, 1862.

vii Stokes, *Discoveries in Australia,* 1:143–44.

viii Flinders, *Voyage to Terra Australis,* 2:235, 236.

ix Wills and Wills, *Successful Exploration,* 211.

Chapter 14

i Wills and Wills, *Successful Exploration,* 213–214.

ii Wills and Wills, *Successful Exploration,* 231.

iii J. G. Macdonald, *Journal of J.G. Macdonald,* 33–34.

iv Wills and Wills, *Successful Exploration,* 213.

v Stokes, *Discoveries in Australia,* 304.

vi Jackson, *Australian Exploration Expedition of 1860,* 223.

vii *Burke and Wills Exploring Expedition* (Melbourne, 1861), 33.

viii Flinders, *Voyage to Terra Australis,* 2:172.

Chapter 15

i Wills and Wills, *Successful Exploration,* 301.

www.ingramcontent.com/pod-product-compliance
Lightning Source LLC
Chambersburg PA
CBHW061133010526
44107CB00068B/2920